The Harcombe Diet®
Phase 1 Recipe Book

Sugar-free, nut-free, gluten-free, mainly low-carb recipes

very best wishes

Zoë + Andy

Published by Columbus Publishing Ltd 2019
www.columbuspublishing.co.uk

ISBN 978-1-907797-68-2
Rev 20190903

Cover design by Andy Harcombe

COLUMBUS PUBLISHING

Contents

Introduction

When we started this project over ten years ago, we had no idea how popular this way of eating would become and how people across the world would embrace the simple concept of 'Just Eat Real Food'.

Our first recipe book, published in 2008, is still immensely popular and it contains over 200 recipes that are simple and quick to make, using basic ingredients that are available in most supermarkets and corner shops. It's a real recipe book for everyday living.

Our second recipe book – Lunchbox Recipes – was in response to an increasing number of people wanting some inspiration for lunches on the go. People no longer want to only eat healthily at home, they want to be healthy all the time. Lunchbox Recipes provides the framework to enjoy quick, easy and nutritious meals for busy people. The simple concept of mixing a main option, a salad option and a sauce/dip allows for a huge number of meal variants to be made, satisfying even the most creatively demanding gastronome.

When creating Lunchbox Recipes, we realised that many of the meals that we eat through choice are wheat-free, dairy-free, nut-free, gluten-free and sugar-free (genuinely sugar-free, not sugar-substituted). They weren't designed to be this way, but have turned out to be so as a result of the staple foods that we have in our house.

As more people have adopted The Harcombe Diet as a way of life, we have learnt that people sometimes want a quick 're-start', and they use Phase 1 as a secret tool to drop a few pounds or a clothes size in a week.

This recipe book takes the lead from Lunchbox Recipes and all the recipes are sugar-free, nut-free and gluten-free. They are all Phase 1 friendly.

Most of the recipes are new and not previously published. We have, however, included a couple of all-time favourites that newcomers and old-timers alike enjoy time and again.

We hope you'll enjoy trying them out and making your own variants from them.

To your very good health…

Zoë and Andy

Chapter 1

About The Harcombe Diet®

The Harcombe Diet® came about following Zoë's interest in weight loss and years of research. Her first books, '*Why do you overeat? When all you want is to be slim*' and '*Stop counting calories and start losing weight*' explained why we crave food and what we need to do to overcome these cravings, as our failure to manage cravings can ruin any diet.

People who bought Zoë's books started to communicate with each other on social media and it was those early adopters who coined the name 'The Harcombe Diet'. When the early books were reprinted, we decided to rename and brand them under their adopted name, and it has stuck and grown ever since.

Most people reading this book will be familiar with The Harcombe Diet®, and we thank you for your support over the years. For 'newbies', welcome! We hope that your health, and weight, will benefit from a return to eating wholesome, real food, in preference to some calorie-restricted fad.

For anyone not familiar with the diet, theharcombediet.com website will give you the headlines, and the books mentioned above, or '*The Harcombe Diet for men*', or '*The Harcombe Diet 3 step plan*' will give you full details of the three phases of the diet. The website and books also provide headlines and details respectively, about the three conditions, (Candida, Food Intolerance and Hypoglycaemia), which the diet is designed to address. Zoë came across the literature describing how these conditions drive food cravings years ago. They were little known conditions then. Nowadays, gut flora, food intolerances and low blood glucose, feature in diet and health news on a daily basis.

As this is a Phase 1 recipe book, we'll look into Phase 1 of The Harcombe Diet in a bit more depth. Chapter 7 lists the foods that you can eat and summarises the Phase 1 'rules'.

Phase 1

Phase 1 of The Harcombe Diet is your secret weapon for whenever you want a quick reboot, and you'll likely drop a few pounds/a clothes size in the process. The record weight-loss during the first 5-days is a massive 17lbs, and 5-10 lbs is quite common.

By design, Phase 1 is genuinely sugar-free, nut-free, and gluten-free and so is perfect if you suffer from food intolerance to any of these common ingredients. Phase 1 is essentially dairy-free as well – milk, cream and cheese are all avoided. The one dairy item allowed is Natural Live Yoghurt (NLY), as many people with lactose intolerance are fine with NLY and it is helpful for one of the conditions (Candida). If you know that you're *not* OK even with NLY, avoid this in the recipes.

Phase 1 can be as short as five days, long enough to rid your body of any lingering food and to get your cravings under control. However, if you know that you suffer quite badly from one or more of the three conditions, you may need to stay on Phase 1 for longer, maybe a few weeks. Some people, especially those with quite a bit of weight to lose, choose to stay on Phase 1 longer still, as they find it the optimal phase for keeping cravings at bay and dropping pounds.

During Phase 1, you'll mainly be eating meat, fish, eggs, poultry, salads and vegetables and Natural Live Yoghurt (the full 'allowed' list is in Chapter 7). These can be enjoyed to satiety. The foods restricted in quantity are brown rice, quinoa and oats. You can use herbs and spices to flavour your food and drink water, decaffeinated drinks and herbal teas.

You'll be eating three main meals a day and you'll only be snacking if you really need to (you should eat at meals to ensure that you don't need to snack before the next one). There are no portions to measure. You won't be hungry and you won't have to count calories, points or syns. Honest!

While all of the recipes in this book are designed for Phase 1, for those doing Phase 2 there are plenty of 'fat meals.' We know that fat meals are popular among Harcombe followers – we tend to find them to be more nutritious and filling. (The website and books can explain 'fat meals' too.)

That's enough about Phase 1 for now – let's get started!

Chapter 2

Getting started

Blitz your kitchen

You will find Phase 1 of The Harcombe Diet much easier to do if you have done some preparation. The most important part of that preparation is to remove anything from your environment that might tempt you. If you don't have junk options to hand, you simply can't reach for them if you get any cravings, or if you're bored, or if you're about to do something from pure habit.

You should diligently work through your food cupboards and fridges and **throw out all of the following**.

Snacks:
Biscuits, cakes, cookies, crisps, confectionery, ALL snack bars, sweets, sugared fruit, dried fruit.

Grains & Cereals:
Bread, cereals (especially branded ones), wheat, flour, croissants, white pasta.

Drinks:
Energy drinks, sports drinks, soft drinks, diet soft drinks, juices (fresh and carton), flavoured water, anything soy based.

Cooking ingredients/spreads:
Bottles of mayonnaise, ketchup, brown sauce; anything that contains 'trans-fats' or 'partially-hydrogenated fats', all margarines, all low-fat spreads, anything that claims to lower your cholesterol.

Misc. condiments:
Sugar in all its forms (white, brown, cane etc.), jam, pickles.

And in the freezer:

Burgers that you've had since last year's Barbeque, all ready-meals, ice creams, ice lollies, etc

We've heard people say that this is a waste and you should give the food away to friends instead. Do you have any friends that you dislike enough to give junk to?!

Now restock your larder

We've looked to keep the recipes in this book simple to make and to store, so that you can make them without the need for specialised equipment or ingredients.

In the kitchen you'll need little more than an oven and a blender, a baking tray here and there, a good quality frying pan and some heavy-duty saucepans.

There may be a handful of ingredients that need a bit of looking for, but the majority you will be able to find in your local supermarket or grocer, if they are not already in your larder cupboard.

We recommend keeping the following staples at home and now that you've cleared out your kitchen, you'll have plenty of room for them.

Herbs and spices:

Cayenne pepper, cumin seeds, peppercorns, sea salt, garlic, coriander seeds, mixed herbs, paprika, turmeric, chilli powder and flakes.

Larder items:

Olive oil, sesame oil, white wine vinegar, rice flour, brown rice, quinoa, red/green lentils, balsamic vinegar, Dijon mustard, Harissa paste, Tabasco.

Tinned produce:

Tomatoes, tuna/salmon, kidney beans, chickpeas.

For the fridge:

Bell peppers, mixed lettuce leaves, tomatoes, onions (white and red), Natural Live Yoghurt (NLY), cheddar cheese, butter.

Other staples/freezer items:

Eggs, mince meat, chicken pieces, pork chops, selection of fish, frozen vegetables.

Some preparation time

Cooking real meals from scratch does, we admit, take a bit of planning and time. Time that we think we don't have with our hectic modern lifestyles. However, with a bit of thought, prioritisation and organisation this time can be minimised and you can be eating delicious and nutritious meals instead of grabbing a quick, industrial packaged ready-meal.

This book is about putting in a bit more effort to prepare something really special, so that you feel you've had a great meal. It takes a lot less effort than you'd think and you may even find that you enjoy knocking up quick and tasty meals for you and your family or friends.

Most recipes in this book are very simple to make and most can be pre or part-cooked in bulk for chilling or freezing, so that you can have your very own ready-meal when you are short of time to cook from scratch.

Of course, the recipes are not limited to Phase 1 meals only. They can form the perfect basis for any meal, picnics or snack.

For a typical main meal, we estimate that most recipes should take no more than about half an hour to prepare and serve (although cooking time may be a few hours if slow roasting or using a slow-cooker). For a breakfast suitable for a king, you're looking at around 5-10 minutes, well worth setting that alarm a few minutes earlier for. You'll reduce these times further with practise and you can always save time by having a main dish for an evening meal, which you can then reuse for the next couple of days. For example, go for a slightly larger than usual pork joint for a slow roast one evening and you'll have leftovers for lunches for the next couple of days and a cold-meat salad for an evening meal.

As with everything in life – you'll get out of this what you put in and we so hope that you enjoy the putting in as much as the getting out and feel encouraged to start being a bit more creative and adventurous with your meals.

The book is structured in four sections:

• Breakfasts

• Mains

• Soups, starters & light bites

• Side dishes & sauces

We've intentionally not included desserts, as you shouldn't need them as part of Phase 1. Make sure you fill up on the main course and enjoy the natural sweetness and flavours that your taste buds will begin to re-learn.

And finally, don't forget the rest of the family. All the recipes in this book are suitable for children and adults alike, whatever their age and whether or not they need to lose weight.

Chapter 3

Breakfasts

The debate is open as to whether breakfast is the most important meal of the day. Some people advocate skipping breakfast completely, which is something that you may choose to do as you progress with your journey on The Harcombe Diet. However, for Phase 1, we recommend that you try to make breakfast one of your three meals a day, so that you don't get hungry mid-morning and succumb to the cravings that will likely follow.

In recent decades, breakfasts have become a quick bowl of cereal or a slice of toast, often laden with some sugary substance (like jam or honey). These undoubtedly give you a blood-sugar high to get you going in the morning but, unfortunately, they soon lead to a blood-sugar low, which then has you thinking about a sandwich mid-morning.

Far better, we think, to start the day with a healthy 'fat' breakfast that will nourish you and keep you satiated through to, and past, lunchtime. We're talking eggs, bacon, butter and vegetables cooked in a variety of ways.

Some Harcombe followers take our 'breakfast is just another meal' mantra to another level and they have been known to eat curry, steak, pork chops, fish, meatballs etc. These are, of course, great foods to eat at anytime of the day, including breakfast, and we do encourage you to experiment with what works for you.

For the purpose of this book, however, we're going to be sticking to more traditional options for breakfast. The quantities are suggestions only based on what Andy eats. If you need to change the number of eggs/slices of bacon to keep you satiated through to lunchtime, then vary the quantities to suit your need.

A final note on breakfast: We often hear people say that they have no time to cook bacon and egg in the morning. Most of the recipes in this section can be made in under five minutes and if you're serious about improving your health and reducing your weight, we think that is a very small investment in time in the morning. Just set your alarm five minutes earlier.

In this Chapter:

- *The perfect fat breakfast*
- *Simple bacon & eggs*
- *Poached eggs (v)*
- *Asparagus scramble (v)*
- *Sautéed greens & nested eggs (v)*
- *Omelette with red pepper (v)*
- *Breakfast 'pizza', with chorizo*
- *Egg cupcakes*
- *Bacon & leek scramble*
- *Oatmeal 'smoothie' (v)*
- *Salmon & chive omelette*

(v) indicates recipes suitable for vegetarians.

The perfect fat breakfast

The perfect start to any day is the dish commonly known as "The Full English". The real "Full English" can include bacon, eggs, sausages, black pudding, tomatoes, baked beans and fried bread, making it a fat storing concoction with unnecessarily added wheat and sugar. For our Phase 1 version we can have any of the following:

- Bacon: Ideally get your meat from the local butcher – best for your community and for your health. The butcher's meat is hard to beat for quality and reduced chance of added ingredients. Choose bacon that is not smoked, sweetened or processed in any unnecessary way. Cured bacon is fine – that's the natural drying/preserving process for meat. Real bacon should look pale in colour and it will not naturally have a long shelf life. If in any doubt, use any slice of pork from the leg or rib instead of bacon. It's just pig & egg at the end of the day. Bacon can be grilled or fried in butter or olive oil.

- Eggs: (provided of course that you are tolerant to eggs) – scrambled, fried (in butter or olive oil), poached, boiled eggs & crudité soldiers etc. Choose the best eggs that you can source and afford.

- Steak, Pork, Chicken or any other pure meat, if you fancy it.

- A few mushrooms and tomatoes fried in olive oil or butter.

- If you can get pure meat sausages from the butcher, with meat and animal products, but no wheat or other carb fillers, these will be fine to have with your fat breakfast. If not, they should be avoided

Avoid:

- All carbohydrates, other than tomatoes or mushrooms. No bread, no baked beans etc.

- All sauces e.g. tomato sauce, ketchup, brown sauce etc. – as these are all laden with sugar and often other refined carbohydrates too.

The "Middle Eastern" breakfast is also a great fat meal. Go for a selection of cold meats and hard-boiled eggs with yoghurt based or spicy dips. For Phase 2, cheese slices can be added if you are ok with dairy.

Here are some basic Phase 1 versions of our favourite fat breakfasts:

Simple bacon & eggs

Ingredients (per person)

2-3 rashers of bacon

2-4 eggs

Knob of butter

Freshly ground black pepper

This is Andy's daily breakfast. We get up, walk the dog and we've barely got back in before Andy is sizzling up his bacon and then adding the eggs. He makes an espresso while all this is happening and then he's ready to face the day a few minutes later. It does amuse us that people are surprised that he's happy with the same breakfast every day when they have cereal every day!

Method

1 Heat a frying pan to a warm heat and add the bacon rashers. Cook them for 2-3 minutes on each side, in their own fat, and then transfer them to a plate and keep them warm under a grill.

2 Melt a knob of butter in the frying pan and, when it begins to bubble, crack the eggs into the butter. Cook for about 3 minutes until the whites become opaque, or longer if you prefer a firmer yolk.

3 Serve immediately on the warmed plate and then grind some pepper over the eggs

Poached eggs (v)

Ingredients: serves 1

25g mixed salad leaves, chopped

½ red pepper, finely sliced

1 tablespoon olive oil

200ml water

Knob of butter

2 eggs

Freshly ground black pepper and sea salt

Poached eggs are one of the simplest, yet most difficult, dishes to master. The secret to success is in getting the water to the right temperature before adding the eggs.

Method

1 Place the salad leaves on a medium plate and add the finely sliced red pepper. Drizzle olive oil over the salad and put it to one side.

2 Add the water to a frying pan and heat to boiling point. Add the knob of butter and then reduce the heat until the water occasionally bubbles.

3 Crack the eggs into the boiling water and tease the whites towards the yolks to keep them in an egg shape. Cook for 3-4 minutes, making sure that you keep the eggs moving in the bubbling water.

4 Remove the eggs from the pan with a slotted spoon and place them on the ready prepared salad. Season to taste and serve immediately.

Asparagus scramble (v)

Ingredients: serves 2

1 tablespoon butter

1 bunch asparagus, about 6 stalks, trimmed and chopped

2 teaspoons dried mixed herbs or 4 teaspoons of fresh herbs (basil, chives, oregano, tarragon, marjoram etc.)

4 large eggs

Freshly ground black pepper and
sea salt to season

Did you ever notice that your urine smells 'funny' after you've eaten asparagus? Not everyone notices this and that's because not everyone produces a smell and not everyone is able to detect the smell. You will need to be both a producer and a detector of 'asparagus wee' to have noticed this. There are a number of compounds in asparagus that might be responsible for the odour. The chief suspect is something called asparagusic acid, which is thought to protect young asparagus shoots from parasites.

Method

1 Melt the butter in a medium frying pan and toss in the chopped asparagus. Cook for 3 minutes.

2 Add all the herbs and seasoning and give the whole lot a good stir. Fry on a medium heat, stirring frequently for a further 3 minutes until the asparagus softens

3 Whisk the eggs in a bowl with a fork and then pour them over the ingredients in the pan. Give the mixture a good stir and cook for a further 2-3 minutes, stirring frequently to ensure that the mixture doesn't become an omelette, until the eggs are cooked.

4 Spoon onto hot plates and enjoy with fresh pepper and a good pinch of sea salt.

Sautéed greens & nested eggs (v)

Ingredients: serves 2

1 tablespoon butter

1 onion, finely chopped

1 clove garlic, finely chopped (optional)

1 bunch, (approximately 75g) Swiss chard, washed and chopped

1 bunch kale (approximately 75g) washed and chopped

A good few pinches of dried marjoram,

Freshly ground black pepper and sea salt to season

4 large eggs

Method

1 Melt the butter in a frying pan then add the onion and garlic and lightly fry for 2 minutes.

2 Add the chard and kale and sauté for a few minutes then add the marjoram.

3 Sauté for a further 5 minutes until the greens have reduced down and have softened.

4 Use a spoon to make four wells in the veg and crack an egg into each one. Season with sea salt and freshly ground pepper.

5 Reduce the heat and cook for a further 5 minutes until the egg whites become firm.

6 Spoon onto hot plates and serve immediately.

Omelette with red pepper (v)

Ingredients: serves 1

2 tablespoons butter

½ onion, finely chopped

½ red pepper, coarsely chopped

2-3 eggs

Fresh ground black pepper and sea salt to season

This is one of our favourite super quick breakfasts, or light lunch, when we are pushed for time. We can go from start to plate in under five minutes. Most people can find that in their schedule for such a tasty and nutritious start to the day.

Method

1 Melt the butter in a small frying/omelette pan, and add the onion and pepper. Fry for about 2 minutes until the onion and pepper start to soften.

2 Whisk the eggs in a small bowl and pour over the onion and pepper. Give the eggs a good stir so that the onion and pepper are nicely distributed. Season with some Freshly ground black pepper and sea salt and cook over a medium heat for about 3 minutes.

3 The next part depends on personal taste. I like my omelettes slightly undercooked so I flip them out of the pan and onto a warm plate at this point. If you like your omelette well-done, just flip the omelette over in the pan and cook for a further 2 minutes and then serve onto a warm plate.

Breakfast 'pizza' with chorizo

Ingredients: serves 2

1 chorizo sausage, around 250g, sliced

1 medium onion, chopped

1 clove garlic, finely chopped

4-6 eggs

Fresh ground black pepper and sea salt to season

This isn't really a 'pizza', it's more of an omelette, really, but calling it a pizza is a great way to get the kids in the house to think they're having a real breakfast treat.

Chorizo is a type of pork sausage. Traditionally it uses natural casings made from intestines, so it's perfect for ticking the 'real food sausage' box. It is typically made from pork, pork fat, garlic, smoked paprika and salt, so those are the only ingredients needed.

Method

1 Toss the sliced chorizo, chopped onion and garlic into a heavy frying pan and cook on a medium heat until the sausage is nicely brown.

2 Whisk the eggs in a bowl and then pour into the frying pan. Cook for about 3 minutes until the eggs become firm then either flip the 'pizza' in the frying pan and cook for a further 3 minutes or finish off under a hot grill for 3-4 minutes.

3 Transfer to a warmed plate, cut in two and eat hot.

TIP *You can also cook this in advance and eat cold for breakfast or as a lunchbox main dish.*

Egg cupcakes

Ingredients: serves 4

8 eggs

1 onion, finely chopped

1, small courgette, finely diced

½ red pepper, diced

½ yellow pepper, diced

6-8 slices of bacon

Sea salt and black pepper to taste

Method

1 Pre-heat the oven to 175°C, 350°F, Gas 4.

2 Crack the eggs into a large mixing bowl and whisk well

3 Add the onion courgette, peppers and pre-cooked bacon to the mixture and mix well.

4 Spoon the mixture into pre-greased muffin tins (6 or 12 cavity) to fill the cavities just over half way.

5 Bake for about 30 minutes, until brown

TIP *For a non Phase 1, or if you're ok with dairy, sprinkle some grated cheese on top before baking.*

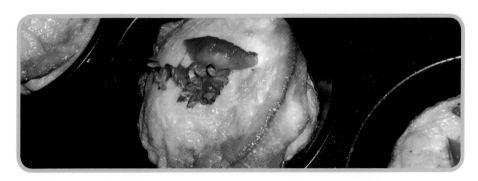

Bacon & leek scramble

Ingredients: serves 2-4

2 leeks

3 tablespoons butter

4 slices bacon, chopped

4-6 eggs

Sea salt and black pepper to taste

Method

1 To prepare the leeks, trim the darker green tops off the leeks and slice the lighter green/ white bottom section in half lengthwise. Then slice crosswise into thin strips so that you end up with thin, half circle slices.

2 Melt 2 tablespoons of butter in a frying pan and sauté the leeks for 8-10 minutes until very soft and just turning brown.

3 While the leeks are cooking, quickly fry the bacon bits in a hot frying pan until they are nicely browned, then transfer them to a plate and keep them warm under a grill. Turn the heat down to low.

4 Whisk the eggs with some sea salt and pepper and then pour into the frying pan used for the bacon with the remaining butter. Cook the eggs slowly, stirring occasionally, until they are softly cooked through. Be careful not to overcook them, you don't want them all dry and hard.

5 Spoon the scrambled eggs onto a warm plate then spoon on the leeks and top with bacon bits. Serve hot.

Oatmeal smoothie (v)

Ingredients: serves 4

4 tablespoons oatmeal

150ml Natural Live Yoghurt (NLY)

Forget complex juicing and sugar laden fruit smoothies, this is as quick as it gets to make a nutritious start to the day, or a quick lunch on the go. It really only takes 30 seconds. Try it.

Method

1 In a food processor, blend the oats for ten seconds.

2 Add the NLY and blend for a further 10 seconds.

3 Scoop out and serve.

TIP *For a similarly quick Phase 2 option, add some strawberries or blueberries to the NLY and blend.*

Salmon & chive omelette

> **Ingredients: serves 2**
>
> *4-6 eggs*
>
> *1 tablespoon freshly chopped chives*
>
> *25g butter*
>
> *100g pre-cooked salmon*
>
> *Sea salt and freshly ground black pepper*

You can buy pre-cooked salmon in most supermarkets – or make extra at dinner one evening. If pressed, use a tin of salmon.

Method

1 Crack the eggs in a mixing bowl and beat with a fork until the yolk and white are nicely combined. Season well with salt and pepper and stir in the chopped chives.

2 Melt the butter in a small frying pan and pour in the eggs. Then flake the salmon over the mixture and give it a quick stir with a plastic spoon to make sure all the ingredients are well distributed.

3 Cook over a medium heat for about 5 minutes until the eggs are cooked through.

4 Flip out, fold in half onto a warm plate and then cut it in two (or eat it for one if really hungry).

5 Serve with a green salad.

Chapter 4

Mains

When you eat your main meal of the day will depend on your lifestyle and personal preferences. Irregular working patterns demands on your time and when you like to eat will influence when you prepare and eat your main meal.

Whatever time or place you choose to have your main meal, please make time to sit down in a relaxed fashion to eat and enjoy your meal.

There is no fixed portion size for each main item and you should adjust the quantities to suit what you need to get you through your busy day and to your next meal.

We all get times when our blood sugar gets a bit low, we get the shakes and we reach for a snack. Having some healthy snacks available in your fridge or lunchbox helps to make sure that you make good choices for your health, rather than succumbing to a sugar laden cereal bar or bar of confectionery.

Like all the recipes in this book, these dishes can be made in advance and will usually keep for five days or more in a fridge (depending on the original freshness of ingredients).

In this Chapter:

- *Haddock with fennel butter*
- *Hake with lemon & dill*
- *Salmon Provencal*
- *Baked cod & tomatoes*
- *Marinated salmon steak*
- *Curried quinoa (v)*
- *Vegetarian chilli (v)*
- *Toasted quinoa tabouleh (v)*
- *Spicy aubergine & egg tagine (v)*
- *Peppered steak*

- Liver & onions
- Homemade beef burgers
- Steak with tomato salsa
- Herby meatballs with tomato sauce
- Lamb with oregano & basil
- Roast lamb with garlic
- Tandoori chicken
- Spicy chicken
- Cumin & coriander lamb
- Marinated lamb steaks
- Spiced roast lamb
- Roast lamb & rosemary
- Minced meat kebabs
- Stuffed peppers with minced beef
- Roast chicken & vegetables
- Moroccan roast chicken
- Devilled kidneys
- Steak & horseradish 'cream'
- Harissa lamb with yoghurt
- Beef, chicken or pork teriyaki
- Chilli chicken (devilled chicken)
- Moroccan stew (v)
- Grilled lemon & thyme pork chops
- Chimichurri chicken
- Pork & fennel satay
- Stuffed chicken breasts
- Salmon with basil sauce
- Chicken Korma
- Sizzling chicken wings
- Tuna with fennel
- Cod with garlic spinach
- Cod Bolognese
- Fish hotpot
- Spiced fish casserole

- Bacon & haddock casserole
- Beef & tomato casserole
- Beef with peppers
- Braised topside (of beef)
- Braised Cajun ham
- Spicy lamb hotpot
- Savoury lamb hearts
- Shepherd's pie with celeriac topping
- Quick curried chicken
- Brown rice risotto (v)
- Macaroni rice pasta with Tomato Sauce (v)
- Veggie Goulash (v)

(v) = vegetarian

Haddock with fennel butter

Ingredients: serves 4

4 haddock fillets (size to suit you – 200-300g as a guide)

50g butter

1 lemon

3 tablespoons chopped fresh fennel

Haddock is a salt water fish and it would have been a favourite for granny to serve on fish Fridays. Like cod, it's a chunky fish, which is why it has been a 'fish and chip' shop classic for years. It doesn't fall apart when cooked, but you can slice down the fish easily while eating. Take care at the fishmonger to get fresh haddock and not smoked. Smoked haddock could be eaten alone, as a breakfast or with a salad for lunch.

Method

1 Pre heat the oven to 225°C, 425°F, Gas 7.

2 Melt a quarter of the butter in a frying pan and quickly fry the haddock for 2 minutes on both sides.

3 Transfer the fish to an oven-proof dish, squeeze the juice from the lemon over the fish and pop the lemon rind on top of the fish. Bake in the oven for 20 minutes.

4 5 minutes before the fish is cooked, melt the remaining butter in the frying pan and add the chopped fennel. Cook over a low heat for 5 minutes.

5 To serve, transfer the fish to warmed plates. Then pour the juice from the fish into the frying pan with the butter and fennel. Quickly bring to the boil and then pour the juices over the fish.

6 Serve hot with some French beans or a side salad.

Hake with lemon & dill

Ingredients: serves 4

4 hake fillets

Drizzle of olive oil

1 lemon, juice and rind of

A few sprigs of fresh dill, chopped

Method

1 Pre-heat the grill to its highest setting.

2 Brush the fillets both sides with a little olive oil. Then place the fillets skin side up on a roasting tray and pop under the grill for 5 minutes, until the skin is crispy.

3 Turn the fillets over and grill on high for a further 3 minutes. Then turn the heat down to half.

4 Remove from the heat and sprinkle the fillets with the grated lemon rind and chopped dill. Then pop back under the reduced temperature grill for a further 4 minutes.

5 Transfer to a warmed plate and squeeze over the lemon juice. Serve hot with French beans.

TIP *Swap the dill for a teaspoon of chilli flakes to make this a dish with a kick.*

Salmon Provençal

Ingredients: serves 4

2 shallots, coarsely chopped

1 green pepper, deseeded and coarsely chopped

1 x 400g tin of chopped tomatoes

1 tablespoon each of fresh tarragon, chives and tarragon

Juice of ½ lemon

4 salmon fillets

Olive oil for cooking

This is a variation on a classic recipe that we discovered while on holidays in the Canaries. The Provencal sauce is traditionally served cold by the side of the salmon but in the canaries, they make a kind of stew with similar ingredients. It's delicious.

Method

1 Pre-heat the oven to 200°C, 400°F, Gas 6.

2 Pour some olive oil in a saucepan and lightly fry the shallots and green pepper for 3-4 minutes. Pour in the tomatoes and bring to the boil. Then stir in the herbs and reduce to simmer.

3 Meanwhile, lightly fry the salmon fillets both sides in some olive oil just enough to brown them. About 2 minutes each side, as a guide.

4 Transfer the salmon fillets to an oven-proof dish, squeeze over the lemon juice and pour the sauce from the saucepan evenly over the fish. Bake for about 20 minutes.

5 Serve hot with your favourite green vegetables.

TIP 1 *Replace the tin of tomatoes with an equal volume of fresh ones for a more extravagant version.*

TIP 2 *Replace the salmon with cod or hake.*

Baked cod & tomatoes

Ingredients: serves 4

4 cod pieces

250g cherry tomatoes, quartered

1 tablespoon fresh basil, chopped

Olive oil for cooking

Sea salt and freshly ground pepper

Cod is a saltwater fish. There are three species of cods: Atlantic, Pacific and Greenland. That makes cod a cold-water fish too. Cod flesh is whiter than most other fish because its muscle tissue is not built for speed. Cod swim around quite slowly with their mouths open to eat anything (plant or animal) in their path. The slow cod are easily caught by trawlers, which is why we are the cod's main prey.

Method

1 Pre-heat the oven to 200°C, 400°F, Gas 6.

2 Heat a small amount of olive oil in a heavy saucepan and lightly fry the cod on both sides. Then transfer to an oven-proof dish.

3 Sprinkle the tomatoes and then the basil over the cod pieces and season with sea salt and freshly ground pepper. Bake in the pre-heated oven for 20 minutes.

4 Serve hot with French green beans.

TIP *For a Phase 2 dish if you are ok with dairy, sprinkle some grated cheese to step 3 before baking.*

Marinated salmon steak

Ingredients: serves 4

Small bunch of fresh coriander

2 cloves garlic

Sea salt and freshly ground pepper to season

3 tablespoons olive oil

4 salmon steaks

Juice of ½ lemon

Marinating the salmon before cooking greatly adds to the flavours that are infused and changes a simple piece of fish into a delicious feast.

Method

1 Put the coriander, garlic, salt and pepper in a pestle and mortar and pour over the olive oil. Then bash everything together until you have a very rough paste.

2 Place the salmon steaks in a dish and rub the marinade mix into the flesh. Cover with cling film, chill and leave to marinate for an hour.

3 Place the salmon steaks on a baking tray and grill under a very hot grill, skin up first and then turned over, for 5-6 minutes each side, until the steaks are nicely browned on the outside, while remaining pink on the inside.

4 Transfer to warm plates, squeeze a little lemon juice over each steak and sprinkle with some freshly chopped coriander.

TIP 1 *Add a chopped chilli to the marinade mix to spice it up a little.*

TIP 2 *Try this recipe with cod or haddock, instead of salmon.*

Curried quinoa (v)

Ingredients: serves 4

4 tablespoons coconut oil

400g quinoa

3 tablespoons of curry powder

500ml vegetable stock

1 white onion, finely chopped

250g mixed vegetables – mange tout, baby sweet corn, chopped French beans etc

100g Natural Live Yoghurt (NLY)

Fresh mint or coriander

Quinoa (pronounced keen-wah) is a naturally gluten-free substance. It's usually called a grain, but technically it's a seed from the chenopodium quinoa plant. It is a rare plant food in that it contains all the essential amino acids that we need to consume in our diet, although not in sufficient amounts to qualify as a complete protein. Animal foods provide complete protein easily – the plant world doesn't.

Method

1 In a heavy frying pan, heat half the coconut oil and lightly fry the quinoa for 2-3 minutes. Then stir in the curry powder and fry for a further 2 minutes.

2 Pour in the stock and quickly bring to the boil. Then reduce the heat to simmer. Cook for a further 10 minutes until all the fluid is absorbed into the quinoa. Transfer to a serving bowl and keep warm.

3 Heat the remaining coconut oil and lightly fry the onion for a minute. Then add the mange tout and other vegetables. Cook on a medium heat for 5 minutes, stirring occasionally until softened.

4 Mix the quinoa and vegetables in the serving bowl, pour the NLY in a neat dollop in the middle and sprinkle with the fresh mint or coriander.

Vegetarian chilli (v)

Ingredients: serves 4

Olive oil for cooking

2 large onions, coarsely chopped

3 cloves garlic, crushed

2 medium courgettes, chopped

2 large red peppers, cored, seeded, diced

3 hot chillis, seeded, finely chopped

1 x 400g tin Italian plum tomatoes, coarsely chopped, including liquid

1 tablespoon ground cumin

2 tablespoons chilli powder or chilli flakes

2 tablespoons chopped fresh chopped oregano

1 teaspoon fennel seeds

1 head broccoli, chipped into florets

150g baby sweetcorn

Zest of 1 lemon

3 tablespoons lemon juice

Large bunch chopped fresh coriander

Salt and freshly ground black pepper to taste

Although the ingredient list is long, this is a really simple dish to make and improves with re-heating. You can serve it with brown rice as a main meal or as a side dish as an alternative to Ratatouille. The amount of chilli is a guide only and you should adjust for your (and your guests') taste.

Method

1 Heat 3 tablespoons of oil in a casserole dish and lightly fry the onions on a medium heat for about 5 minutes. Add the garlic and cook for a further minute. Then add the courgettes, peppers and chillis. Cook for a further 4-5 minutes, stirring occasionally.

2 Turn down the heat and stir in the tomatoes, herbs and spices. Add the broccoli and sweet corn and give the whole mixture a good stir. Pop the lid on the casserole dish and simmer for 30 minutes.

3 Just before serving, stir in the lemon zest and juice and the fresh coriander.

4 Serve with brown rice and some natural live yoghurt.

TIP 1 *Add a drained tin (400g) of unsweetened kidney beans at step 2 to make this a Phase 2 (carb) dish.*

TIP 2 *Make in advance and reheat to serve as a side dish.*

TIP 3 *Serve onto a baked potato to make a quick and filling Phase 2 (carb) meal.*

Toasted quinoa tabouleh (v)

Ingredients: serves 4

400g quinoa

500ml vegetable stock

125g cherry tomatoes, quartered

2 cloves garlic, crushed

1 red onion, finely chopped

6 spring onions, sliced

Bunch of fresh mint or coriander, chopped

50ml olive oil

Juice of 1 lemon

Sea salt and freshly ground pepper to season

You can eat this dish as a vegetarian meal, or use it as a side dish alongside some of the other meals in this book. It can also be chilled and eaten cold, which is great for your lunchbox.

Method

1 Pour the quinoa into a heavy frying pan and dry fry for about 10 minutes, stirring frequently, until the quinoa is lightly 'toasted'. Pour the stock over the quinoa, season well and bring to the boil, then reduce to simmer for 15 minutes until the stock is absorbed into the quinoa.

2 While the quinoa is cooking, mix together the tomatoes, garlic, red onion, spring onions and herbs.

3 For the dressing, whisk together the olive oil and lemon juice and season with salt and pepper.

4 Mix the tomato mixture with the cooked quinoa and pour the olive oil and tomato dressing over.

5 Serve at room temperature or chill for a lunchbox or salad.

Spicy aubergine & egg tagine (v)

Ingredients: serves 4

3 medium aubergines, cubed

3 medium peppers, (red, green and yellow) thinly sliced

2 medium onions, chopped

2 cloves garlic, crushed

4 large tomatoes, chopped

5 tablespoons olive oil

2 tablespoons spice mix (1 teaspoon each of: cumin; cinnamon; chilli powder; coriander; paprika; turmeric and fennel, and ½ teaspoon each of ginger and cardamom pounded in a pestle and mortar)

500ml vegetable stock

1 tablespoon harissa paste

4 large eggs

½ cup coarsely chopped fresh parsley, for garnish

6 lemon wedges, for garnish

A tagine is traditionally a North African stew, cooked in a special shaped earthenware pot. We use a heavy casserole dish and you can also use a slow cooker. The secret to the delicious mix of flavours is to cook this dish slowly, ideally the day before you intend to eat it.

Method

1 Pre-heat the oven to 135°C, 275°F, Gas 1.

2 Put the aubergine, peppers, onions, garlic and tomatoes in a heavy casserole dish or slow cooker. Pour over the olive oil and sprinkle the spice mix. Then give the mixture a good stir.

3 Add the vegetable stock and harissa paste and stir again. Pop the casserole in the oven and cook for 3-4 hours.

4 Form 4 shallow wells in the mixture and crack an egg into each one. Return to the oven and bake for a further 15 minutes, until the eggs are cooked.

5 This classic North African dish would normally be served with couscous, but this isn't gluten-free, so serve with brown rice.

Peppered steak

Ingredients: serves 2

2 steaks, size and type to suite your preference and hunger

Sea salt and freshly ground black pepper

1 teaspoon olive oil

2 cloves garlic

1 tablespoon butter

If you're ever in a classy restaurant, one of the best ways to test the quality of the chef is to ask for a steak. One of the most difficult things to judge is the perfect rare vs. medium vs. medium-rare steak. We've suggested a guide below, but you'll soon master the perfect pan heat and cooking time to get your steak just how you like it. Many of the top restaurants now use the 'sous vide' method to cook the perfect steak and then they just quickly seal it up before serving.

Method

1 Allow the steak to get to room temperature before cooking.

2 Season both sides of the steak with plenty of sea salt and freshly ground pepper, pressing the spices into the meat.

3 Heat the olive oil in a heavy bottomed frying pan until it separates and just begins to smoke. Gently place the steak in the pan and cook on one side for a minute. Turn the steak over and cook the other side for a minute. Both sides should now be sealed. Toss the garlic clove into the pan.

4 Continue to flip sides, cooking for 2 minutes each time until your steak is cooked to your liking. This would be, roughly, 2-3 minutes for rare, 3-4 minutes for medium, 4-6 minutes for well done.

5 Remove from the heat and add the butter to the pan. Flip the steak in the butter so that it's well coated. Leave to stand in a warm place for 3-4 minutes before serving.

6 To serve, give the butter and juices a quick stir then place the steak on a warmed plate and spoon over the butter sauce. Pop the garlic on top of the steak. Serve with a salad or green beans.

Liver & onions

Ingredients: serves 2

2 onions, finely sliced

1 tablespoon butter

350g liver (lamb, pig, ox), sliced

This was a weekly treat when I (Andy) was growing up and it remains one of my favourite meals to this day. The onions add a lot of moisture to what, if overcooked, can be quite a dry dish. Resist the temptation to cook the liver 'well-done' and this classic dish will be even more special.

Method

1 Slowly fry the onions in the butter for about 10-12 minutes, stirring occasionally until they just begin to brown. Transfer to a plate and keep warm.

2 Add the liver to the pan and lightly fry for 2-3 minutes on each side, until the liver is nicely brown on the outside and pink on the inside (test by slicing one piece with a sharp knife).

3 Return the onion to the pan and quickly bring back to temperature over a high heat for a minute. Stirring all the time so as not to burn the onion or the liver.

4 Serve on a warmed plate with bubble and squeak (see page 113).

Homemade beef burgers

Ingredients: makes 4-8 burgers

500g mince beef

1 medium onion, very finely chopped

1 clove garlic, crushed

2 teaspoons dried mixed herbs

1 egg, whisked

Sea salt and freshly ground black pepper

Mince (ground) beef is really good value when bought from your butcher and you can be pretty sure that it will be good quality mince too. This is a basic recipe to start with and you can experiment with different kinds of mince (lamb, pork, turkey etc.) and flavourings (curry, spices etc.).

Method

1 Mix the mince, onion, garlic and herbs in large mixing bowl using your hands to knead the mixture.

2 Add the whisked egg, salt and pepper and knead further until you have a nice consistent mixture.

3 Split the mixture into 4, or 8 for smaller burgers, and form small, firm, balls in your hands. Then press the balls onto a tray to make burger shaped patties.

4 The burgers can be cooked immediately by grilling, frying or on a Barbeque or frozen for future use.

TIP 1 *Freeze separately on a baking tray before packing together. This will ensure that the burgers don't solidify into a single lump.*

TIP 2 *For a Phase 2 variation (if you're OK with dairy), just before serving sprinkle each burger with some grated cheese and a sliced onion and grill for 2-3 minutes until the cheese is brown. Top with a slice of tomato.*

Steak with tomato salsa

Ingredients: serves 2

2 steaks, size and type to suite your preference and hunger

Sea salt and freshly ground pepper

100g cherry tomatoes

4 spring onions

A few tablespoons of water

Method

1 Allow the steak to get to room temperature before cooking.

2 Season both sides of the steak with sea salt and freshly ground pepper, pressing the spices into the meat.

3 Chop the cherry tomatoes into quarters and slice the spring onions. Mix in a bowl and put aside.

4 Heat a heavy bottomed frying pan and dry fry the steaks to your liking. Start with just a minute each side to seal the steaks and then turn every 2 minutes. Then transfer the steaks to warmed plates.

5 To make the salsa, tip the tomatoes and spring onions into the frying pan, add a little water and cook them for 2-3 minutes in the juices from the steaks, making sure you scrape any meat residue from the frying pan (to include this in the salsa for extra flavour).

6 Pour the salsa over the steaks and serve immediately.

TIP *You can spice up the salsa by adding half a chopped chilli or a dash of Tabasco.*

Herby meatballs with tomato sauce

Ingredients: serves 4

For the meatballs

450g minced beef

1 onion, finely chopped

1 clove garlic, crushed

3 teaspoons dried mixed herbs

Sea salt and freshly ground pepper

1 egg, beaten

For the tomato sauce

400g tin tomatoes, chopped

1 tablespoon butter

1 small onion, halved

Method

1 Pre-heat the oven to 200°C, 400°F, Gas 6.

2 Put the minced beef, onion, garlic, herbs, salt and pepper in a mixing bowl and thoroughly mix together. Then mix in the beaten egg.

3 Take a small amount of the mixture and make approximately 20 golf ball sized meat balls, placing each one them on a baking tray.

4 Pop in the oven and roast for about 30 minutes, until the meat browns. Remove from the oven to cool.

5 To make the tomato sauce, put the tomatoes, butter and onion in a small saucepan, bring quickly to the boil then cover and simmer for 30 minutes.

6 Remove and discard one half of the onion and then quickly blitz the remaining ingredients with a hand blender until you get a smooth sauce.

7 To Serve, divide the meatballs equally and then spoon over the tomato sauce.

TIP *Use lamb mince instead of beef for a very different taste.*

Lamb with oregano & basil

Ingredients: serves 4

3 tablespoons olive oil

1 tablespoon fresh chopped oregano

1 tablespoon fresh chopped basil

1 clove garlic, crushed

Sea salt and freshly ground pepper

8 lamb chops (or 4 double 'Barnsley chops')

Method

1 Mix the olive oil, herbs, garlic, salt and pepper in a small bowl.

2 Place the lamb chops in a shallow dish and pour half the mixture over the chops. Turn the chops over and pour the remaining marinade over them. Cover with cling film and leave to marinate for about 8 hours. Tip, make the marinate in the morning and the chops will be perfectly ready to cook by tea time.

3 To cook, remove the lamb from the marinade and fry over a medium heat for about 5 minutes on each side. Just before serving, pour the marinade into the frying pan and give the whole lot a good stir, until the marinade is warmed through.

4 Transfer the chops to warm plates and spoon over the marinade sauce. Serve with your favourite green vegetables.

TIP 1 *Try using different cuts of meat for this dish – lamb steaks, leg, shoulder etc.*

TIP 2 *Make an alternative marinade using chopped rosemary and thyme.*

Roast lamb with garlic

Ingredients: serves 4

1 shoulder of lamb, approximately 1.5-2kg

2 tablespoons olive oil

12 garlic cloves, unpeeled

Sea salt and freshly ground pepper

Method

1 Pre-heat the oven to 175°C, 350°F, Gas 4.

2 In a frying pan, warm the olive oil and toss in the garlic. Give the cloves a good stir so that they are well covered in the oil and then pour the cloves and olive oil into a roasting dish. Season with salt and pepper.

3 Place the shoulder of lamb on top of the garlic and roast in the oven for about 2 hours.

4 Remove from the oven, cover with aluminium foil and allow to rest for 20 minutes before carving.

5 Serve onto warmed plates with a few cloves of garlic on top of each serving. The garlic cloves will be deliciously sweet and can be eaten straight from their skin.

Tandoori chicken

Ingredients: serves 4

4 pieces of chicken – breast, leg, quarter (if really hungry)

200ml Natural Live Yoghurt (NLY)

3 tablespoons Tandoori mix

(To make your own Tandoori mix, simply crush/mix the following in a pestle and mortar
3 teaspoons each of ground ginger and coriander; 1 teaspoon each of ground
cumin, paprika, black pepper, turmeric, ground nutmeg, cloves and cinnamon)

Method

1 Slash the chicken pieces and then place them in a non-metalic, oven-proof dish.

2 Mix together the NLY and Tandoori mix and pour over the chicken, making sure that the
pieces are well covered and are worked into the slashed meat. Cover with cling film
and marinate in the fridge for 8 hours.

3 Pre-heat the oven to 175°C, 350°F, Gas 4. Remove the cling film and pop the whole dish
in the oven and roast for about 30 minutes, until the chicken is cooked through.

4 Serve immediately or chill and use in your lunchbox or have with a salad.

TIP 1 Try using lamb instead of chicken.

TIP 2 Make a large batch of the Tandoori mix and keep
it in an airtight container for future use.

Spicy chicken

Ingredients: serves 4

1 tablespoon chilli powder

1 tablespoon cumin

1 tablespoon olive oil

4 pieces of chicken

This chicken dish is equally tasty served hot or cold. We've used chicken pieces here, but you can use a whole chicken and just roast it.

Method

1 Mix the chilli powder, cumin and olive oil in a mixing bowl.

2 Dip each piece of chicken in the mixture and make sure that each piece is well coated. Transfer each piece to a roasting dish and then pour any remaining olive oil and spice mix over the chicken pieces.

3 Heat a grill to medium and them pop the chicken under the grill and cook for 10 minutes. Turn the pieces over and cook for a further 10 minutes. The exact cooking time will depend on the size of the chicken pieces so test that the juices run clear before serving.

TIP *Instead of grilling, prepare the chicken in advance and barbecue.*

Cumin & coriander lamb

Ingredients: serves 4

1 tablespoon cumin

1 tablespoon coriander seeds

1 tablespoon olive oil

8 lamb chops

100ml Natural Live Yoghurt (NLY)

This is another super-simple mix that changes a simple grilled piece of meat into a deliciously tasty meal.

Method

1 Grind the cumin and coriander in a pestle and mortar and mix in the olive oil.

2 Dip each lamb chop in the mixture and make sure that each piece is well coated. Transfer each piece to a roasting dish and then pour any remaining olive oil mix over the chops. Cover and marinate for an hour, longer if you can wait

3 Pre-heat the grill to hot. Transfer the chops to a roasting dish and pop them under the grill for 5 minutes. Turn the chops over and grill for a further 5 minutes. The chops should now be pink on the inside. Cook for a few more minutes on each side if you prefer them well done.

4 Remove from the grill and transfer to warmed plates.

5 Spoon a dollop of NLY on each chop and serve with your favourite greens.

TIP *Try with chicken, instead of lamb*

Marinated lamb steaks

Ingredients: serves 4

Juice of 1 lemon

2 tablespoons olive oil

2 tablespoons freshly chopped oregano or rosemary

2 onions, finely sliced

4 lamb steaks

Sea salt and freshly ground pepper

This is a slow-roast dish that can also be made using a slow-cooker. We suggest marinating the steaks first but if you're short on time, you can just load everything into a slow-cooker and set to run on low.

Method

1 Mix the lemon juice, olive oil and oregano in a bowl.

2 Place a steak in a non-metalic dish, cover with some of the onion slices and then drizzle some of the marinade over it. Place a second steak on top and repeat for the remaining steaks. Cover with cling film and marinate for 4-8 hours.

3 To cook, line a roasting dish with aluminium foil and transfer the steaks, along with the onions and marinade to the roasting dish. Wrap the aluminium foil around the steaks and fold to seal. Pop in a moderate oven, 150°C, 300°F, Gas 2 for 2 hours. Serve hot with favourite greens.

Spiced roast lamb

Ingredients: serves 4

1 lamb joint, about 2kg. e.g. leg, shoulder, rack, saddle

4 garlic cloves, halved

2 tablespoons olive oil

Juice of 1 lemon

1 tablespoon paprika

1 tablespoon mustard

½ teaspoon dried thyme

½ teaspoon dried rosemary

Method

1 Make 8 incisions in the lamb and push half a clove of garlic into each one.

2 Mix the olive oil, lemon juice, paprika, mustard, thyme and rosemary in a bowl and then rub all over the lamb joint. Leave to marinate for an hour.

3 Pre-heat the oven to 175°C, 350°F, Gas 4.

4 Transfer the lamb to a roasting dish and pop in the oven for about 2 hours. Then remove from the oven, cover with aluminium foil and allow to stand in a warm place for 20 minutes before carving.

5 Serve hot with roasted vegetables or your favourite greens.

Roast lamb & rosemary

Ingredients: serves 4

½ leg of lamb, approximately 2kg

Handful of fresh rosemary

12 cloves garlic (left in their skin)

Being Welsh, Andy's supposed have grown up on lamb and mint sauce, but he's always preferred rosemary as his herb of choice with lamb.

Method

1 Pre-heat the oven to 175°C, 350°F, Gas 4.

2 Make 3 or 4 incisions in the lamb and press some fresh rosemary into each one.

3 Line a roasting dish with aluminium foil and place the cloves of garlic on the foil. Place the lamb joint on top of the garlic and wrap the foil around the lamb.

4 Pop the lamb in the oven and cook for about 1 ½ hours. Then, open up the foil and roast for a further 30 minutes so that the fat is nicely browned.

5 Remove from the oven, cover the joint back up with the foil and allow to rest in a warm place for 30 minutes. Then carve and serve hot.

TIP 1 *The roast garlic can either be served alongside the meat and eaten as a vegetable (it becomes deliciously mushy and sweet) or crushed into the meat juices to make a delicious sauce.*

TIP 2 *Use a shoulder of lamb for a cheaper alternative.*

Minced meat kebabs

Ingredients: serves 4

450g lamb mince

450g beef mince

1 large onion, finely chopped

2 cloves garlic, crushed

1 tablespoon ground cumin

Juice of ½ lemon

Sea salt and freshly ground pepper

One myth about eating real food is that it's expensive. First think of all the foods that you no longer buy: sweets; crisps; biscuits; cakes; fizzy drinks; branded foods; ready meals etc. Then think of all the super nutrient dense foods that are cheap: offal; tinned fish; trays of eggs; misshaped vegetables; plain oats etc. One of the cheapest meat options is mince – it can be one third or even one quarter of the price of steak. The cheapest mince is also the higher fat option, which you will find more satiating and therefore need less of. 15% fat mince can be two thirds or even half the price of lean (5% fat) mince. Shop smart!

Method

1 Put all the ingredients in a large mixing bowl and knead until thoroughly mixed.

2 Take a small handful of the mixture and shape into a small ball around a skewer. Repeat so that you have 3-4 balls on each skewer and make as many skewers as you can, probably 8-10.

3 Cook the skewers on a barbeque or under a hot grill for about 10 minutes, until nicely browned.

4 Serve hot with a tossed salad for a Phase 2 fat meal, or on a bed of brown rice if you fancy a substantial Phase 1 meal.

Stuffed peppers with minced beef

Ingredients: serves 4

450g beef mince

1 large onion, finely chopped

2 celery sticks, finely chopped

1 clove garlic, crushed

1 teaspoon crushed coriander

Sea salt and freshly ground pepper

4 red peppers, or mixed colours

Fresh coriander leaves to garnish

Method

1 Fry the beef mince in a frying pan for about 10 minutes, stirring occasionally until it is nicely browned. Then, spoon out the meat to a dish, leaving the fat in the frying pan.

2 Add the onion, celery and garlic to the frying pan and cook in the beef fat for about 5 minutes, until the onion becomes translucent.

3 Add the mince back to the frying pan and give the whole mixture a good stir. Add the coriander and seasoning and cook on a low heat for about 30 minutes.

4 Meanwhile, pre-heat the oven to 190°C, 375°F, Gas 5.

5 Slice the top off the red peppers and remove the seeds. Slice a very small slice off the bottom of the pepper so that it will stand upright on a baking tray. Chop up all the leftover pieces of pepper and stir into the mince mix.

6 Spoon the meat mix into the pepper cavities, pressing down the mixture with the back of a spoon. Place the peppers on a baking tray and pop in the oven for about 30 minutes.

7 Serve hot with a green salad and a sprinkling of freshly chopped coriander.

Roast chicken & vegetables

Ingredients: serves 4

1 whole chicken

1 lemon, quartered

Sprig of fresh thyme

1 aubergine, cut into 2cm cubes

1 red pepper, deseeded and quartered

1 green pepper, deseeded and quartered

1 fennel bulb, trimmed and quartered

2 red onions, quartered

6 cloves garlic (left in skin)

4 tablespoons olive oil

This is such a simple, yet somehow extravagant looking dish that takes just 10 minutes to prepare.

Method

1 Pre-heat the oven to 200°C, 400°F, Gas 6.

2 Pop the lemon quarters and thyme inside the chicken and place breast side down on a roasting dish.

3 Arrange all the vegetables around the chicken in the roasting dish and drizzle the olive oil over the chicken and vegetables.

4 Roast in the oven for 30 minutes. Then, remove from the oven, turn the chicken over so that it's breast side up and give the vegetables a good stir. Pop back in the oven and cook for a further 1½ hours, until the chicken skin is nicely browned and the juices run clear.

5 Serve hot with your favourite greens.

Moroccan roast chicken

Ingredients: serves 4

4 pieces of chicken (leg, breast, quarter)

2 shallots, finely chopped

2 cloves garlic

1 sprig fresh coriander

1 sprig fresh parsley

1 teaspoon each of sea salt, paprika, cumin

Large pinch of cayenne pepper

Juice of 1 lemon

Moroccan cuisine is characterised by plenty of vegetables, flavour and colour, with meat highly valued. In less affluent households, where meat is less available, the delicious thick sauces are mopped up with bread. Cooking is often slow – roasting or stewing – to fully develop the flavour and also to soften meat.

Method

1 Pre-heat the oven to 200°C, 400°F, Gas 6.

2 Put the shallots, garlic, herbs and spices and lemon juice in a large pestle and mortar and crush everything together until you have a coarse paste.

3 Place the chicken pieces on a roasting dish and rub the paste all over the chicken. Then, pop in the oven and roast for about an hour, until the juices run clear from the chicken.

4 Serve hot with a selection of vegetables.

Devilled kidneys

Ingredients: serves 4 as a starter, 2 for main

Large knob of butter

1 shallot, finely chopped

2 cloves garlic, finely chopped

½ teaspoon cayenne pepper

12 lamb's kidneys, halved

Devilled kidneys are a traditional breakfast dish that can equally be enjoyed as a quick lunch or supper.

Method

1 Melt the butter in a heavy frying pan and lightly fry the shallot and garlic until the shallot becomes clear.

2 Stir in the cayenne pepper and then add the kidneys. Cook for about 3 minutes on each side until they are brown on the outside and still slightly pink in the middle.

3 Serve hot on their own or with some cauliflower rice to soak up the juices.

Steak & horseradish 'cream'

Ingredients: serves 2

2 of your favourite steaks (rib-eye, rump, sirloin)

Sea salt and freshly ground pepper

1 tablespoon olive oil

For the horseradish 'cream'

1 tablespoon grated fresh horseradish

50g Natural Live Yoghurt (NLY)

1 tablespoon chopped fresh chives

Horseradish is a member of the Brassicaceae family (which includes broccoli and cabbage, but also includes mustard and wasabi). It's a root vegetable, which has little flavour until it is grated or mashed and then the pungent taste bursts out making it far more like its mustard and wasabi 'siblings.' It is often served with beef joints, as a Sunday roast. It can be used to enhance a cheap joint. In this recipe, it's used to make a pricey steak a really special meal.

Method

1 Season the steaks well with salt and freshly ground black pepper,

2 Heat the olive oil in a frying pan until it just begins to smoke and then add the steaks. Quickly seal both sides and then cook for a further 3-5 minutes on each side to suit your preference (rare, medium, etc). Then, remove the steaks from the pan and leave to stand on a warm plate.

3 To make the horseradish cream, mix the grated horseradish, NLY and chives to make a smooth cream.

4 Serve each steak with a dollop of horseradish 'cream' along with a mixed salad or some green beans.

Harissa lamb with yoghurt

Ingredients: serves 4

1 shoulder of lamb

2 teaspoons hot Harissa paste

(many shop varieties are sugar and wheat free)

Lamb is one of my (Andy's) favourite meats and this ultra-simple recipe adds a delicious middle-eastern bite. You can cook it this way as a variant for a regular roast dinner or serve as a snack or as part of a Tapas supper.

Method

1 Score the lamb joint with a sharp knife and spoon the Harissa paste over the meat, rubbing into the scores with the back of the spoon. Wrap in aluminium foil and allow to marinate for about an hour.

2 Pop the joint, still wrapped in foil, in a medium oven, 150°C, 300°F, Gas 2 for 2-3 hours.

3 Remove from the oven and allow to rest for half an hour. Then open up the foil and pop under a medium grill for 10 minutes to crisp up the skin.

4 Carve or pull the meat off the bone – it should just fall away after the slow cooking, and serve hot with your favourite greens, or a nice bowl of thick Natural Live Yoghurt.

Beef, chicken or pork teriyaki

Ingredients: serves 2-4

For the marinade

1 teaspoon ground ginger

1 teaspoon freshly ground black pepper

5 tablespoons strong Tamari soy sauce

2½ teaspoons chilli puree (or a couple of fresh chillies finely chopped)

500g beef, chicken or pork chunks

For the stir-fry

Olive oil for frying

A selection of vegetables of your choice. For example: white or green cabbage, shredded carrots beetroot, red/yellow/green peppers thinly sliced, courgette, cauliflower or broccoli or florets, mange tout peas etc

Method

1 Stir together all the marinade ingredients. Then, add the meat and stir well. Leave for a few hours, or ideally overnight, in the fridge.

2 Add a few tablespoons of olive oil to a wok or large pan. Stir-fry the vegetables for 5-10 minutes until they are as you like them.

3 Meanwhile, fry the meat in a different pan in a little olive oil until cooked, pouring any leftover marinade onto your vegetables.

4 Add the marinated meat/poultry to your vegetables and cook together for a few minutes until everything is hot, pouring any leftover marinade over the vegetables. If there is not much liquid, add a splash of water.

5 This is so delicious you will probably not want rice – just add more vegetables to your stir-fry.

Chilli chicken (devilled chicken)

Ingredients: serves 2

2 chicken quarters

Juice of ½ lemon and the remaining lemon

2 tablespoons olive oil

2 cloves garlic, chopped in half

1 teaspoon chilli flakes

This was my (Zoë's) favourite main meal for quite some time. Andy would serve the chicken in a pasta style bowl and pour some of the juices from the chicken over the stir-fried vegetables. They tasted great to start with, from his wok technique, but the chicken/lemon/olive oil and slightly spicy juices on top made them quite special. Then the chicken would be falling off the bone having been long cooked and yet the top skin would be blackened and crispy. Yum!

Method

1 Pre-heat the oven to 150°C, 300°F, Gas 2.

2 Place the chicken pieces on a piece of aluminium foil and squeeze the lemon juice over the chicken. Place the remaining piece of lemon with the chicken.

3 Drizzle the olive oil over the chicken pieces and sprinkle with the chilli flakes. Add the garlic and wrap the whole lot up in the foil.

4 Place in the oven and cook for 2 hours.

5 Remove from the oven and leave to rest for 15 minutes. Then open up the foil and place under a grill and grill on a medium heat until nicely brown.

6 Serve warm with stir-fried vegetables.

Moroccan stew (v)

Ingredients: serves 4

For the spice mix

1 tablespoon each of ground cumin, black peppercorns, allspice mix, grated fresh ginger, paprika

½ tablespoon each of fennel seeds and coriander seeds

½ teaspoon each of cinnamon and turmeric

Good pinch of sea salt

For the stew

1 tablespoon olive oil

2 onions, coarsely chopped

2 cloves garlic, crushed

1 red pepper, deseeded and coarsely chopped

1 green pepper, deseeded and coarsely chopped

1 x 400g tin tomatoes, chopped

1kg approximately of mixed vegetables, e.g. squashes, carrots, courgettes, beans etc

250ml vegetable stock

1 ½ tablespoons spice mix

Method

1 To make the spice mix, put all the ingredients in a pestle and mortar and bash until you have a consistent mixture.

2 Heat the olive oil in a large saucepan and lightly fry the onions, garlic and peppers for about 5 minutes.

3 Add all the remaining ingredients and give the mixture a good stir until all the ingredients are nicely mixed together.

4 Bring quickly to the boil and then reduce to simmer for 30 minutes, until the squash is just turning soft.

5 Serve hot with brown rice for a Phase 1 meal or a Phase 2 carb meal.

TIP *Replace the 1kg vegetables with diced lamb, beef or chicken for a non-veggie version.*

Grilled lemon & thyme pork chops

Ingredients: serves 4

Juice and grated rind of ½ lemon

2 garlic cloves, crushed

½ teaspoon sea salt

½ teaspoon chopped fresh thyme

4 large, thick pork chops

Thyme is one of the most versatile herbs in the kitchen. It goes well with most meats – whether plain joints or chops or in stews. It is one of the main herbs used in bouquet garni, which gives many French dishes their striking flavour. Thyme goes well with many other herbs – especially lemon and indeed there are lemon thyme varieties, which have been cultivated. It is a hardy herb, so it can withstand hot ovens for some time. It doesn't get exposed to much heat in this dish, but it will make a significant difference to the natural flavour of pork.

Method

1 Mix the lemon juice and grated rind, garlic, salt and thyme in a small bowl and give everything a quick stir to make a light sauce.

2 Place the pork chops on a plate and pour over the sauce. Cover with cling-film and leave to marinate for about an hour.

3 Pre-heat the grill to very hot and then grill the chops for about 5 minutes each side, so that they are nicely brown. Turn down the heat and cook for a further 5 minutes on each side until they are cooked through.

4 Serve hot with your favourite vegetables or a green salad.

Chimichurri chicken

Ingredients: serves 4

4 large chicken pieces

For the sauce

50g fresh chopped parsley

50g fresh chopped oregano

2 garlic cloves, crushed

½ teaspoon cumin

Juice of ½ lime

4 tablespoons olive oil

Large pinch sea salt

Chimichurri is a green sauce with Argentinian origins. It's traditionally served on beef, but adds an equally delicious bite to chicken.

Method

1 To make the sauce, place the parsley, oregano, garlic and cumin in a bowl and blitz with a hand blender for a few seconds. Then, whisk in the lime juice and olive oil and season with a good pinch of sea salt.

2 Pre-heat a grill to high and grill the chicken until the skin is crisp and the meat is cooked through, turning twice.

3 Transfer the meat to a warmed plate and spoon the sauce all over the chicken pieces. Serve hot with a green salad or chill and serve cold (or save it for your lunchbox).

TIP *This sauce is also delicious with steak – the Argentinian way.*

Pork & fennel satay

Ingredients: serves 4

2 teaspoons each of cumin seeds, fennel seeds and turmeric

Zest and juice of 1 lemon

6 tablespoons of coconut cream

½ teaspoon sea salt

600g, approximately, of pork, cubed

Satay is a traditional dish in Indonesia and Malaysia. It consists of small cubes of meat placed on a skewer and served with a spiced sauce. The sauce usually contains peanuts, but not our version, as we leave mix-foods to Phase 3.

Method

1 Crush the cumin and fennel seeds in a pestle and mortar and add the turmeric. Add the salt and lemon zest and juice and then whisk in the coconut cream.

2 Place the pork in a dish and pour over the sauce. Give it a good stir so that the pork is well covered by the sauce. Cover and chill for 3-4 hours, overnight if possible.

3 Thread the pork cubes onto skewers (aim for eight, two each) and then grill or barbeque, for about 15-20 minutes, until the meat is cooked through.

4 Serve hot with your favourite vegetables or a green salad. Pork and rice also go well together if you're doing the five-day Phase 1 and are OK mixing.

Stuffed chicken breasts

Ingredients: serves 4

1 tablespoon olive oil

½ onion, finely chopped

½ red pepper, thinly sliced

1 chilli pepper, deseeded and sliced

2 handfuls fresh spinach, washed and coarsely chopped

2 cloves garlic, crushed

Juice of ½ lemon

4 chicken breasts

Don't forget to buy chicken breasts with the skin on, for extra flavour and nutrients and because you are going to crisp up the skin just before serving. Skinless chicken breasts are more expensive than those with the skin on at our butchers. People pay a premium for wasting real food!

Method

1 Pre-heat the oven to 150°C, 300°F, Gas 2.

2 In a mixing bowl, thoroughly mix the olive oil, onion, peppers, spinach, garlic and lemon juice until you have a coarse paste.

3 Cut a slice along the middle of each chicken breast and stuff ¼ of the paste into each chicken.

4 Place the chicken pieces in the centre of a sheet of aluminium foil and wrap the foil around the chicken to create a tight seal.

5 Place in the oven and cook for 2 hours. Then open up the aluminium foil and finish off the chicken under the grill to crisp the skin.

6 Serve hot onto warmed plates, spooning the juice over the chicken.

Salmon with basil sauce

Ingredients: serves 4

4 salmon steaks

4 tablespoons olive oil

250g fresh basil

Juice of 2 lemons

Sea salt and freshly ground black pepper

We have left meat and fish portion sizes to your discretion. The amount of fat/protein that you need at each meal will depend on your age, gender, size, activity levels, nutrient requirements, what else you eat during the day and many other factors. As an example, a 200g portion of salmon provides 100% of the daily vitamin B12 requirement, as well as excellent amounts of other B vitamins, fat soluble vitamins, the mineral phosphorus and omega-3 essential fats.

We are advised to eat oily fish, such as salmon, 2-3 times a week. This should be the minimum intake, as recommended amounts are needed daily, not weekly. Fish can be expensive and salmon might be a rare treat, but sardines, mackerel, herrings, the 'catch of the day' and other highly nutritious fish are often more affordable.

Method

1 Place the salmon steaks skin side up on a grill pan and place under a hot grill. Grill for 2-3 minutes, until the skin is charred and then turn over and cook for a further 5 minutes until lightly browned.

2 Meanwhile, to prepare the basil sauce, remove the basil leaves and whizz them in a food processor or hand blender for a few seconds. Then, add the lemon juice and seasoning and whisk with a hand whisk. Continue whisking while slowly pouring in the olive oil. Set aside until ready to use.

3 To serve, place a salmon steak on a warmed plate and pour over some of the basil sauce. Serve with some green beans.

Chicken Korma

Ingredients: serves 4

4 pieces of chicken (legs/breasts/quarters)

4 tablespoons olive or coconut oil

2 onions, finely chopped

2 garlic cloves, crushed

2 teaspoons turmeric

2 teaspoons chopped ginger

2 teaspoons ground coriander seeds

Seeds of 5 cardamom pods

100ml Natural Live Yoghurt (NLY)

Method

1 In a large wok, lightly fry the chicken in your chosen oil for about 10 minutes, turning each piece until nicely brown and well sealed. Then, transfer to a warmed plate.

2 In the same wok, add the onions, garlic, turmeric, ginger, coriander and cardamom seeds and fry for a further 2 minutes. Then, turn off the heat, allow to cool for a few minutes before stirring in the yoghurt.

3 Transfer the chicken pieces back to the wok and give everything a good stir, so that the chicken is well covered by the yoghurt mix. Add a little water if necessary to make the mixture flow.

4 Turn the heat back onto low and simmer for about 15 minutes until the chicken is cooked through.

5 Serve hot with brown rice for a Phase 1 dish or with any vegetables for a Phase 2 fat meal.

Sizzling chicken wings

Ingredients: serves 4

2 tablespoons olive or coconut oil

1 onion, finely chopped

2 garlic cloves, finely chopped

2 teaspoons fresh ginger, finely chopped

2 teaspoons cumin seeds

1 red chilli, deseeded and finely chopped

12 chicken wings

2 teaspoons Tamari soy sauce

Tamari soy sauce is traditionally made with little or no wheat. You should be able to find a variety that is 100% soybean, with no added nasties at all. While soybeans should not be consumed in large amounts (as vegetarians often do), the tiny amount of Tamari soy sauce in this recipe provides each serving barely a trace of the substance. This sauce is fine to use in such small quantities for large flavour in recipes, therefore.

Method

1 Pre-heat the oven to 200°C, 400°F, Gas 6.

2 Heat the oil in a wok and add the chopped onion. Cook for about 5 minutes until it is lightly brown. Then, add the garlic, ginger, cumin and chilli. Stir well and cook for a further minute. Transfer to a warm plate.

3 Add the chicken to the wok and fry in the remaining oil for about 5 minutes, until nicely browned, stirring frequently.

4 Pour the onion and spice mix back into the wok. Then add the Tamari soy sauce and give it a good stir. Then, transfer everything to an oven-proof dish and cook in the oven for 20-30 minutes until the chicken is cooked through.

5 Serve hot with your favourite vegetables, or allow to cool and chill for your lunchbox.

Tuna with fennel

Ingredients: serves 2

2 tuna steaks

2 tablespoons olive oil

Juice of ½ lemon

1 garlic clove, crushed

Sea salt and freshly ground black pepper

2 fennel bulbs, thinly sliced lengthways

Method

1 Place the tuna steaks on a deep plate.

2 Whisk together the olive oil, lemon, garlic, salt and pepper and pour this over the tuna steaks. Cover and marinate for 30 minutes.

3 Heat a griddle pan and cook the sliced fennel bulbs for 5 minutes on each side until they have nice black ridges. Transfer to a warmed plate and pour the marinade from the tuna over them.

4 On the same griddle pan, cook the tuna steaks for about 5 minutes on each side until they too have nice black ridges on the outside, but remain soft and moist on the inside.

5 To serve, place the fennel on a warmed plate and place a tuna steak on top. Finish by pouring the marinade over the tuna. Serve with green beans or a salad.

Cod with garlic spinach

Ingredients: serves 4

3 tablespoons olive oil

3 garlic cloves, crushed

500g spinach – washed and chopped

4 cod fillets

200g cherry tomatoes

Sea salt and freshly ground black pepper

You make like to increase your portion size for white fish, as it isn't as filling as oily fish. This is because white fish, such as cod, is higher in protein and lower in fat than oily fish. Protein is satiating, but fat tends to be even more so and the fat-protein combination in natural meat and fish (i.e. not lean choices) is ideal for keeping hunger at bay until the next main meal.

Method

1 Heat 2 tablespoons olive oil in a frying pan and add the garlic and spinach, cook over a low heat for about 5 minutes until the spinach wilts.

2 Place the cod and tomatoes on a grill-pan. Lightly sprinkle with a little olive oil and season with salt and pepper. Grill under a hot grill for about 5 minutes on each side until the cod lightly browns.

3 To serve, spoon the spinach onto each plate, place a cod fillet on top of the spinach and top off with a few grilled tomatoes.

Cod Bolognese

Ingredients: sevres 4

2 cod fillets

2 tablespoons olive oil

2 cloves garlic, crushed

1 large tomato, finely chopped

25g butter

Juice of ½ lemon

Sea salt and freshly ground black pepper

1 tablespoon chopped parsley

Method

1 Pre-heat the oven to 150°C, 300°F, Gas 2.

2 Drizzle the olive oil over the base of a casserole dish and arrange the cod fillets on top.

3 Sprinkle the garlic and chopped tomato over the fish and then dot with butter. Finish with the lemon juice, salt and pepper.

4 Cover the dish and cook in the oven for about 45 minutes, until the fish is cooked through.

5 Serve onto hot plates with your favourite greens. Better still, Ratatouille would be a perfect accompaniment to cod in terms of flavour and colour.

Fish hotpot

Ingredients: 2 as a main or 4 as a starter

500g white fish (cod, hake, halibut etc), boned and chopped

2 onions, finely sliced

2 large carrots, peeled and sliced

2 sticks celery

6 large tomatoes, sliced

Sea salt and freshly ground black pepper

Bouquet garni

Approximately 1 litre of water or fish stock

Method

1 Pre-heat the oven to 150°C, 300°F, Gas 2.

2 In a heavy casserole dish, build up layers of fish and vegetables, sprinkling each layer with a little salt and pepper. Finish with the bouquet garni.

3 Add the water/fish stock to half cover the contents. Cover and cook in the oven for about an hour.

Spiced fish casserole

Ingredients: serves 2-4

500g white fish (cod, haddock), boned and chopped

1 bay leaf

Juice of ½ lemon

Sea salt and freshly ground black pepper

25g butter

For the spiced sauce

25g butter

½ teaspoon anchovy essence or 1 anchovy, crushed

3 cloves

½ teaspoon chilli powder

400g tin tomatoes, finely chopped

A few dashes of Tabasco

Method

1 Pre-heat the oven to 165°C, 325°F, Gas 3.

2 Chop the fish into bite sized chunks and place in a casserole dish. Add the bay leaf, lemon juice, salt, pepper and dot with butter. Cover and place in the oven and cook for 30 minutes.

3 Meanwhile, make the spiced sauce.

4 Melt the butter in a saucepan. Then add all the other ingredients, stirring as you add them. Bring to the boil then turn the heat down until you just get the occasional bubble. Simmer for about 20 minutes

5 Pour the sauce over the fish in the casserole dish and cook for a further 15-20 minutes.

6 Serve hot in a shallow bowl along with some greens or cauliflower rice.

Bacon & haddock casserole

Ingredients: serves 4

6 slices streaky bacon, chopped

1 large onion, finely chopped

1 teaspoon curry powder

1 250g tin chopped tomatoes

100ml water

2 tablespoons Worcestershire sauce

600g haddock

Method

1 Pre-heat the oven to 165°C, 325°F, Gas 3.

2 Heat a heavy based casserole dish on the hob and fry the bacon in its own fat until crispy. Remove from the pan.

3 Add the onions to the casserole dish and fry them in the bacon fat until they just begin to brown, scraping any bacon bits off the casserole bottom into the onion mix as you stir.

4 Add the bacon back to the casserole dish and mix well with the onions. Add the curry powder, tomatoes, water and Worcestershire sauce and bring to the boil. Then remove half the mixture from the casserole dish.

5 Arrange the fish on top of the mixture that's left in the casserole dish and then pour the other half on top.

6 Cover and cook in the oven for 45 minutes.

7 Serve hot in a shallow bowl along with some greens or cauliflower rice.

Beef & tomato casserole

Ingredients: serves 4

50g good quality beef dripping

1kg beef topside

1 large onion, coarsely sliced

400g carrots, sliced

400g tomatoes, coarsely chopped

1 beef stock cube and 300ml water or 300ml beef bone broth

Sea salt and freshly ground black pepper

This is a hearty and satiating dish that's just perfect for a simple lunch or supper. Serve hot with some mixed, roasted, vegetables for a stress-free alternative to a traditional Sunday roast.

Method

1 Pre-heat the oven to 150°C, 300°F, Gas 2.

2 Heat the dripping in a heavy, thick-based casserole dish. Add the beef and brown on all sides.

3 Add the vegetables to the casserole dish, placing them around the beef joint.

4 In a separate saucepan, dissolve the beef stock in the water and then pour over the beef joint. Alternatively, warm the bone broth and pour over the joint.

5 Season well with salt and pepper, cover and cook in the oven for 3-6 hours.

6 Remove from the oven and allow to rest for 30 minutes before serving.

7 A perfect Sunday roast is best served with simple seasonable vegetables. You have onions, carrots and tomatoes already, so a bit of cauliflower or broccoli would be ideal.

Beef with peppers

Ingredients: serves 4

2 tablespoons olive oil

1kg good quality stewing beef, diced

1 large onion, coarsely sliced

2 cloves garlic, crushed

200g carrots, sliced

1 beef stock cube and 300ml water or 300ml beef bone broth

Sea salt and freshly ground black pepper

1 red pepper, seeded and diced

1 green pepper, seeded and diced

1 yellow pepper, seeded and diced

Method

1 Pre-heat the oven to 165°C, 325°F, Gas 3.

2 Heat the oil in a frying pan and add the meat. Cook until lightly brown and then transfer to a casserole dish. Do the same for the onions and garlic.

3 Place the carrots on top of the beef, onions and garlic in the casserole dish and pour over the stock/broth. Season with salt and pepper and cook in the low oven at for 2-3 hours

4 An hour before serving, remove the casserole dish from the oven and give the stew a good stir. Place the chopped peppers on top and return to the oven for a further 45 minutes.

5 Remove from the oven to rest for 15 minutes before serving.

6 Delicious with cauliflower rice and buttered broccoli.

Braised topside (of beef)

Ingredients: serves 4

25g good quality beef dripping

1-1.5kg beef topside

1 large onion, quartered

400g carrots, sliced

150g (1 medium) turnip, peeled and chopped

3 sticks celery, chopped

1 beef stock cube and 150ml water or 150ml beef bone broth

1 bouquet garni

Sea salt and freshly ground black pepper

Method

1 Pre-heat the oven to 150°C, 300°F, Gas 2.

2 Heat the dripping in a heavy frying pan. Add the beef and brown on all sides.

3 Put all the vegetables into the casserole dish and place the beef joint on top. Add the bouquet garni and pour in the stock. Season well.

4 Place the lid on the casserole dish and cook for 4-6 hours in the low oven.

5 Remove from the oven and allow to rest for 30 minutes before serving.

6 Carve the meat onto a warmed plate and arrange the vegetables around. Serve the sauce as a gravy.

Braised Cajun ham

Ingredients: serves 8

2kg slipper or gammon joint

350ml water

5 tablespoons Cajun spice mix (see p 128)

You can cook a simple boiled ham in just a few hours but creating something truly scrumptious takes a little longer. We think that this is worth the effort. Start with a big joint, as it will disappear fast.

Method

1 Soak the ham in cold water for 15 minutes. Drain the water and rinse the ham in fresh water. Then, place the ham in a casserole dish and half cover with fresh cold water. Place the lid on the casserole dish and cook for 3 hours in a low oven, 150°C, 300°F, Gas 2.

2 Remove the ham from the casserole dish and wrap in aluminium foil. Leave to cool for about 1 hour.

3 Scrape off and discard any 'jelly' and remove any excess fat from the ham. Score the skin of the ham and liberally rub the Cajun spice mix over the ham.

4 Reheat the oven to 190°C, 375°F, Gas 5. Place the ham (in the foil) on a roasting dish and pop in the oven. Cook on a moderate heat for 45 minutes. Remove from the oven, wrap the foil back around the ham and leave to stand for a further 30 minutes.

5 You can now carve and serve the ham warm, or allow it to cool and serve cold. This will have been a labour of love, but well worth it.

Spicy lamb hotpot

Ingredients: serves 4

1kg best end, neck of lamb, diced

2 medium onions, coarsely chopped

1 garlic clove, crushed

1 sticks celery, chopped

3 large tomatoes, coarsely chopped

½ green pepper, deseeded and chopped

½ teaspoon paprika

½ teaspoon mixed spice

50ml water

Salt and pepper

Method

1 Pre-heat the oven to 165°C, 325°F, Gas 3.

2 Heat a frying pan and toss in the diced lamb. Quickly fry and brown it in its own juices. Transfer the meat to a casserole dish.

3 Quickly fry the onions and garlic in the frying pan until they start to turn brown. Add them to the meat.

4 Toss the remaining vegetables and spices into the frying pan and cook for 2-3 minutes. Pour in the water and bring to the boil, stirring the mixture and scraping any bits from the bottom of the frying pan. Pour the mixture over the meat and season well.

5 Place the lid on the casserole dish and cook for 3 hours in the low oven.

6 Serve onto warmed dishes with your favourite vegetables (cauliflower rice is perfect to soak up the juices).

Savoury lamb hearts

Ingredients: serves 4

4 lamb's hearts

2 medium onions, quartered

2 carrots, peeled and coarsely chopped

250ml beef stock or bone broth

For the stuffing

50g butter

1 onion, finely chopped

1 stick celery, finely chopped

Juice and grated rind of 1 orange

½ teaspoon cayenne pepper

Sea salt

1 egg, beaten

Hearts are deliciously flavoursome and cheap. While very meaty in texture, they are not at all what you'd expect from offal – they taste more like a lean steak. Do try them.

Method

1 Pre-heat the oven to 165°C, 325°F, Gas 3.

2 To make the stuffing, melt the butter in a frying pan and add the chopped onion and celery and lightly cook for 2-3 minutes. Add the orange juice and rind, cayenne pepper and salt and give it a quick stir.

3 Quickly bring the mixture to the boil. Then remove it from the heat and mix in the beaten egg.

4 Fill the hearts with the stuffing and, using a wooden skewer, 'stitch' the heart.

5 Put the quartered onions and carrots in a casserole dish and place the hearts on top. Pour in the stock/broth.

6 Place the lid on the casserole dish and cook in the oven for 2 hours.

7 Serve onto warmed dishes with your favourite green vegetables.

Shepherd's pie with celeriac topping

Ingredients: serves 4

1 large cauliflower, coarsely chopped

50g butter

1 tablespoon olive oil

1 small onion, chopped

2 cloves garlic, minced

2 stalks celery, chopped

3 carrots, washed and diced (peeled or not is up to you)

500g minced beef or lamb

200ml chicken stock

1 teaspoon dried rosemary

½ teaspoon dried thyme

Salt & pepper to taste

This may become one of your main meal staples during the week. Make an extra big portion if you want some left over for other meals. It's cheaper than steaks or joints – you can always add more vegetables to make it go further – and it looks so impressive with the slightly browned topping. You may do a double take because it looks so close to the mashed potato version!

Method

1 Pre-heat the oven to 200°C, 400°F, Gas 6.

2 Place the cauliflower in a saucepan and half fill with water. Bring to the boil, place the lid on the pan, lower the heat and simmer for 20 minutes.

3 Meanwhile, heat the oil in a frying pan and lightly fry the onion and garlic, until they just turn a light brown. Add the celery and carrots and cook for a further 2 minutes.

4 Add the minced meat and cook for about 10 minutes, until the meat is nicely browned. Make sure that the mixture is stirred frequently so that it doesn't burn.

5 Stir in the chicken stock, herbs and seasoning and bring the mixture to the boil, then reduce and simmer for a few minutes while you return to the cauliflower.

6 Remove the cauliflower pan from the heat and drain off the water. Lightly mash the cauliflower with the back of a fork until you have a mixture that looks like mashed potato. Add the butter and mash a bit more.

7 Transfer the meat mixture to a baking dish and spread out evenly. Top with the mashed cauliflower and pop in the oven for about 30 minutes, until the cauliflower starts to brown.

8 Serve hot with your favourite greens.

Quick curried chicken

Ingredients: serves 4

1 chicken

2 tablespoons olive oil

1 onion, finely chopped

2 garlic cloves, crushed

2 dessertspoons curry powder

1-2 teaspoons chilli powder

25ml creamed coconut

250ml chicken stock

This is quick to prepare, although the cooking time is longer. When you get home from work, this will only take a few minutes before everything is in the oven or saucepan and then you have time to open the post, feed the cat and close down emails before your dinner.

Method

1 This recipe can be cooked in a saucepan or in the oven. Pre-heat the oven to 165°C, 325°F, Gas 3 if you are going for that method.

2 Joint the chicken and chop the meat into pieces. Heat the oil in a saucepan and lightly brown the chicken bits on all sides. Transfer to a casserole dish or heavy based saucepan.

3 Add the onion and garlic to the frying pan and cook in the oil and juices for 2-3 minutes. Spoon everything over the chicken.

4 Add the curry powder, chilli powder and creamed coconut to the pan, giving them a good stir and scraping any bits stuck to the bottom of the pan to keep them in the mix.

5 Pour in the stock and quickly bring to the boil, stirring frequently.

6 Place the lid on the casserole dish and cook for 1½ hours in the oven. Or, if using a saucepan, bring the curry to the boil, place the lid on the pan and simmer for 30-45 minutes, then reduce to simmer.

7 Serve with brown rice (Phase 1) or cauliflower rice (Phase 1 or 2).

Brown rice risotto (v)

Ingredients: serves 2

200g brown rice, cooked to instructions

Knob of butter for frying

1 medium onion, finely chopped

1 green pepper, deseeded and sliced

1 clove garlic, crushed

4 medium sized tomatoes, coarsely chopped

100g green peas (frozen are fine)

Salt and freshly ground pepper for seasoning

Method

1 Cook the brown rice in plenty of water following the cooking instructions.

2 While the rice is cooking, melt the butter in a frying pan and lightly fry the onion and pepper until they start to soften. Stir in the garlic, tomatoes and peas and cook for a further 5 minutes on a low heat. Stir frequently.

3 Drain the rice and rinse with clean boiling water to remove any of the scum that you get with brown rice. Stir the rice into the vegetables in the frying pan and continue stirring for 2-3 minutes until the mixture is all nicely mixed together.

4 Season well, give a final stir and serve onto warmed dishes.

Macaroni rice pasta with tomato sauce (v)

Ingredients: serves 2

Knob of butter for frying

1 medium onion, finely chopped

1 clove garlic, crushed

1 green pepper, deseeded and sliced

400g tin tomatoes, chopped

100ml vegetable stock

200g courgettes, diced

200g rice pasta (any shape will do)

Salt and freshly ground pepper for seasoning

Fresh basil, approximately 50g, roughly torn

You will be able to find rice pasta in the gluten-free section of most supermarkets. There are quite a few shapes and varieties. We have also found vegetable pasta made in different colours using beetroot (for red), carrot (for orange) and courgettes (for green). You may like to try corn pasta for a change too – the key thing is to avoid the standard wheat pasta options, as they aren't gluten-free.

Method

1 Melt the butter in a saucepan and lightly fry the onion, garlic and pepper until they start to soften. Stir in the tomatoes and stock and quickly bring to the boil. Reduce the heat and simmer for 10 minutes.

2 Add the courgettes to the sauce, season well and simmer for a further 10 minutes until the courgettes start to soften.

3 While the courgettes are cooking in the sauce, cook the rice pasta in plenty of water until just soft, then drain.

4 Spoon the pasta into warmed dishes and spoon the sauce over the pasta. Garnish with some fresh basil and serve immediately.

Veggie goulash (v)

Ingredients: serves 4

Olive oil for frying

1 medium onion, finely chopped

1 clove garlic, crushed

4 carrots, sliced

4 courgettes, sliced

½ small white cabbage, grated

1 tablespoon paprika

½ teaspoon caraway seeds

½ teaspoon mixed herbs

500g tomato juice

300ml vegetable stock

Salt and freshly ground pepper for seasoning

Natural Live Yoghurt (NLY)

Method

1 Heat the oil in a deep saucepan and lightly fry the onion, garlic and carrots for 2-3 minutes. Add the courgettes and cabbage and cook for a further 10 minutes, stirring frequently.

2 Stir in all the herbs and spices – paprika, caraway seeds and mixed herbs – and then pour in the tomato juice and vegetable stock. Stir well and bring quickly to the boil. Reduce the heat and simmer for about 20 minutes until the vegetables are just cooked.

3 Spoon the Goulash into warmed dishes and add a dollop of NLY to each serving.

Chapter 5

Soups, starters & light bites

There is a lot more to salads than a few wilted lettuce leaves, which you used to get as garnish with your pub meal. With a little creativity, salads can make any lunch an exciting and exotic mix of flavours, packed with nutrients. We've listed some of our favourites, which can be made and stored usually for up to five days at any time of the year (check the use-by date, but always do the 'sniff & taste' test).

In this chapter:

- *Roast garlic & butternut squash soup (v)*
- *Chicken liver salad*
- *Sizzling prawns*
- *Salmon steaks with lime & coriander*
- *Simple onion soup (can be v)*
- *Tuna Niçoise*
- *Gazpacho (v)*
- *Grilled tomato soup (v)*
- *Stuffed tomatoes & peppers (v)*
- *Cold beef salad*
- *Egg salad (v)*
- *Egg & Bacon Salad*
- *Warm chicken salad*
- *Egg Mayonnaise (v)*
- *Coronation chicken*
- *Curried chicken salad*
- *Butternut squash, carrot & ginger soup (v)*
- *Swede & turmeric soup (v)*
- *Chef's salad*

Roast garlic & butternut squash soup (v)

Ingredients: serves 4

2 garlic bulbs

Olive oil

A few sprigs of thyme

1 butternut squash, peeled, seeded and diced (keep the seeds)

1 large red chilli, seeded and chopped in half

2 medium onions, chopped

1 teaspoon coriander

1 litre vegetable stock

Sprig of fresh oregano/thyme/rosemary

Don't be put off by the amount of garlic in this recipe. When roasted, it adds sweetness and a bite to this delicious soup.

Method

1 Pre-heat the oven to 200°C, 400°F, Gas 6.

2 Remove the outer skin from the garlic and place all the cloves in some aluminium foil and drizzle with a small amount of olive oil. Add the thyme and seal the foil to make a small parcel. Place the diced butternut squash and chilli on a roasting dish and drizzle with a little oil. Place the garlic parcel alongside. Pop in the oven and roast for 30 minutes. Remove from the oven.

3 In a large saucepan, lightly fry the onions in a little oil until transparent. Squeeze the garlic out of their skins into the saucepan and stir well with the onions. Add the coriander and the roasted squash and chilli and give another good stir.

4 Add the stock to the saucepan and quickly bring to the boil, then reduce and simmer for 15 minutes.

5   While the stock is simmering, spoon the butternut squash seeds onto the roasting dish and pop back into the oven. Roast for 10-15 minutes until they are nicely browned.

6   Remove the soup from the heat and allow to cool slightly. Blend with a hand blender to a smooth consistency then return to the heat to bring back to the boil.

7   Serve into soup bowls and garnish with a few of the roasted seeds and fresh oregano/ thyme/rosemary.

TIP   *For a creamier soup, reduce the stock to 750ml and, just before serving, stir in 150ml cream. While this makes the recipe a 'dairy' option, it's well worth the upgrade if you can tolerate dairy.*

Chicken liver salad

Ingredients: serves 4 as starter or 2 as a light bite

100g green beans

Knob of butter for frying

200g chicken livers, trimmed

200g (approximately) of mixed salad leaves

2 tablespoons lemon juice

If you ever want to win a nutrient competition and you need to choose just one food, choose liver. It's unbeatable for vitamins and minerals. Liver is particularly rich in retinol – the form of vitamin A required by the body. It is so rich in this key nutrient, that granny was right to serve liver once a week and that was seven daily requirements met for the whole week (vitamin A is a fat-soluble vitamin, which means it can be stored by the body).

Method

1 Bring a saucepan of water to the boil and pop in the green beans for 2 minutes. Drain and freshen the beans in cold water and then dry them with kitchen roll.

2 Melt the butter in a hot frying pan and then add the chicken livers. Cook on high for about 5 minutes until they are nicely browned on the outside and still slightly pink on the inside.

3 Arrange the mixed leaves on serving plates and decorate with the beans. Spoon the cooked livers equally onto the leaves.

4 Add the lemon juice to the frying pan and bring to the boil, scraping any bits off the pan. Spoon the mixture over the chicken livers and serve immediately.

Sizzling prawns

Ingredients: serves 4 as a starter or 2 for a light meal

4 tablespoons olive oil

2 dried chillies, deseeded and chopped

2 cloves garlic, finely chopped

16 large prawns, fresh or frozen

Prawns have had a bad reputation because of the cholesterol myth. Like eggs, they were a food naturally rich in dietary cholesterol and thus put on the warning list by people who didn't know better. The fact is that even the so-called father of the cholesterol-diet-heart hypothesis, Dr Ancel Keys, considered that dietary cholesterol made no difference to blood cholesterol levels whatsoever. Prawns should back on the good for you list, therefore, as they are rich in complete protein, omega-3 essential fats and many vitamins and minerals. They are also delicious!

Method

1 Heat the olive oil in a heavy based frying pan and fry the garlic and chillies for about a minute, until the garlic just starts to turn brown.

2 Add the prawns and stir so that they are well covered with the oil. Cook them for 2 minutes on one side, then turn them over and cook them for a further 2 minutes.

3 Transfer to a warmed dish and leave to stand for a few minutes to allow to cool slightly. Serve immediately, or chill and enjoy cold.

Salmon steaks with lime & coriander

Ingredients: serves 2

2 salmon steaks

Handful of fresh coriander

Juice and grated rind of ½ lime

The Harcombe Diet's simplest and easiest meals comprise quality meat, fish and/or eggs and vegetables. Our main meals are invariably a meat chop or a fish portion with whatever has arrived in the vegetable delivery from the villager pensioner that week. Often a few herbs on chicken or some fennel seeds on a pork chop and a plain bit of fat/protein becomes a special meal. This recipe is a classic example of getting a well sourced salmon steak (ideally from your local fishmonger) and adding just a couple of simple ingredients to transform the basic fish into something quite different.

Method

1 Place the salmon skin side down in an oven-proof dish and sprinkle the fresh coriander and lime juice over the steaks. Cover with cling film and leave to marinate for an hour.

2 Turn the steaks over, so that they are skin side up, and pop under a hot grill for 5 minutes until the skin is browned and crispy. Turn the steaks over and grill for a further 5 minutes, until the steaks are nicely browned.

3 Transfer the steaks to warmed plates. Give the juices in the dish a quick stir and spoon equally over the steaks.

4 Serve hot with fresh greens or a salad or chill them and enjoy them cold.

Simple onion soup (can be v)

Ingredients: serves 4

100g butter

1kg onions, finely sliced

1litre beef, chicken or vegetable stock

Salt and freshly ground pepper

This is my (Zoë's) favourite starter when in France. The classic French onion soup is a Phase 3 mix, as it has bread on top of the soup and cheese on top of the bread. It doesn't need the bread – it just needs the melted cheese toasty bit. In fact, it doesn't even need that – the caramelised onions in (our preference) beef stock is such a great mix.

Method

1 Melt the butter in a large saucepan and add all but 100g of the sliced onions. Lightly fry for about 10 minutes until translucent.

2 Pour the stock over the onions, quickly bring to the boil and then reduce the heat and simmer for 20 minutes.

3 Leave the stock to cool for 5 minutes. Then blend to a smooth consistency.

4 Add the remaining 100g of sliced onion to the soup. Bring it back to the boil and simmer for 2-3 minutes. Serve hot.

TIP *For a Phase 2 meal, add some grated Gruyere and toast the topping under the grill until it melts and turns golden.*

Tuna Niçoise

Ingredients: serves 2

2 tuna steaks or 200g tinned tuna

2 tablespoons olive oil

1 clove garlic, bashed

2 eggs, hard boiled, peeled and quartered

200g, approximately, green salad leaves

50g cherry tomatoes, halved

Sea salt and freshly ground black pepper

This is the most basic tuna Niçoise. You can also add lightly boiled green beans and anchovy fillets to the leaves, tomatoes and warm tuna steaks for extra nutrients and variety.

Method

1 Place the tuna steaks in a shallow dish. Mix the olive oil and bashed garlic, pressing the garlic with a fork to extract the juices. Pour the oil over the tuna steaks, cover with cling film and leave to marinate for an hour.

2 Heat a griddle pan to very hot. Remove the tuna steaks from the marinade and cook on the griddle for 2-3 minutes each side, so that they are nicely browned on the outside and still pink in the middle (seared).

3 Arrange the green leaves neatly on a plate or shallow bowl and place a tuna steak in the middle of each one. Arrange 4 egg quarters around each steak and drizzle the olive oil marinade over the tuna and eggs.

4 Arrange the cherry tomatoes similarly around the dish. Sprinkle with sea salt and freshly ground pepper and serve warm.

Gazpacho (v)

Ingredients: serves 4

1 cucumber, peeled, deseeded & chopped

1 onion, chopped

1 red pepper, deseeded & chopped

1 green pepper, deseeded & chopped

Juice of 1 lemon

1 litre of tomato juice, chilled

1 tablespoon olive oil

Sea salt and freshly ground black pepper

This is such an easy recipe for this classic summer soup and it offers all the benefits of raw food. This will be like having a health boosting smoothie for a starter, as it is packed with vitamin C and has useful amounts of other vitamins and minerals from vitamin K to copper.

Method

1 Put all the ingredients in a blender and blend until smooth. You will likely need to do this in batches. Season to taste.

2 Chill in the fridge for 2 hours before serving.

TIP 1 *Peel the cucumber whole; cut lengthways into quarters; slice out the seeds in one knife action and you have a peeled and deseeded cucumber.*

TIP 2 *Add a clove of garlic or a few dashes of Tabasco for extra kick.*

Grilled tomato soup (v)

Ingredients: serves 4

Olive oil for brushing baking trays and frying

1.3kg of ripe tomatoes

2 onions, sliced

3 cloves garlic, crushed

1 fennel bulb, sliced

2 sticks celery, finely sliced

Sea salt and freshly ground black pepper

It takes a bit of time to pre-grill the tomatoes in this recipe, but it really is worth it. The taste of the slightly charred vegetables makes the whole soup really special.

Method

1 Pre-heat the oven to 175°C, 350°F, Gas 4.

2 Cut the tomatoes in half and put them on a baking tray, which has been lightly brushed with olive oil. Grill under a hot grill for about 10 minutes until they start to brown. You may need to do this in batches. Transfer the tomatoes to a large saucepan.

3 Fry the onions, garlic, fennel and celery in a small amount of olive oil until the onions begin to soften. Transfer to a roasting dish and pop in the oven for 30 minutes. Transfer to the saucepan with the grilled tomatoes.

4 Use a hand blender to blend the mixture until smooth.

5 Warm everything in the saucepan (not quite to boiling point), season to taste and serve immediately.

Stuffed tomatoes & peppers (v)

Ingredients: serves 4 as a starter, 2 for a light lunch

2 large bull tomatoes

1 green and 1 yellow pepper, deseeded and cut in half

Olive oil for cooking

2 medium onions, finely chopped

2 cloves garlic, finely chopped

100g long grain brown rice, cooked

1 teaspoon mixed herbs

Sea salt and freshly ground black pepper

Selection of your favourite fresh herbs for garnish – coriander, mint, parsley etc.

Method

1 Pre-heat the oven to 200°C, 400°F, Gas 6.

2 Chop the tomatoes in half and scoop out the flesh. Halve the peppers and clean out the seeds. Place the tomatoes and peppers in a shallow roasting tray.

3 Fry the onions and garlic in a little olive oil for 5 minutes. Remove from the heat and stir in the (cooked) rice, herbs and seasoning. Mix thoroughly with a wooden spoon and then spoon into the tomato and pepper halves.

4 Add a little water to the roasting tray and then pop in the oven for 30-40 minutes, until the edges of the peppers are just turning brown.

5 Remove from the oven, sprinkle with some freshly chopped herbs and serve hot.

Cold beef salad

Ingredients: serves 4

1 clove garlic

1 lemon

50ml extra virgin olive oil

Sea salt and freshly ground black pepper

8 thin slices of rare beef

Rocket salad – approximately 100g

Method

1 Take a small mixing bowl and rub the garlic around the inside.

2 Squeeze in the lemon juice and season well. Slowly pour in the olive oil, while whisking it with the lemon juice, to get a consistent sauce. Leave to stand for 10 minutes.

3 Arrange the beef on a serving dish and pile the salad on top. Drizzle some of the sauce over the arrangement.

TIP *For a Phase 2 fat meal, sprinkle with Parmesan or Emmental shavings when serving.*

Egg salad (v)

Ingredients: serves 4

1 clove garlic, thinly sliced

1 tablespoon olive oil

4 eggs

2 shallots, thinly sliced

1 small red chilli, seeded and thinly sliced

¼ small cucumber, diced

1cm piece root ginger, grated

Juice of a lime or lemon

1 tablespoon Tamari soy sauce

Sea salt and freshly ground black pepper

Large bunch of watercress, chopped

Eggs are a 'superfood' for vegetarians, although they can't compete with meat or fish for most nutrients. This is nonetheless a simple and delicious little snack for lunch, or for your lunchbox.

Method

1 Lightly fry the garlic in the olive oil for 2 minutes. Break the eggs into a bowl and break the yolks. Give them a quick whisk with a fork to just mix the whites and yolks. Add them to the frying pan and fry until firm. Remove from the heat and tip onto a plate to cool.

2 In a mixing bowl, add the shallots, chilli, cucumber, root ginger, lemon or lime juice and Tamari soy sauce and mix well with a fork. Season well and stir again.

3 Arrange the watercress on serving plates. Slice the fried eggs and arrange them on the watercress. Pour the salad mixture over the eggs and serve immediately.

Egg & bacon salad

Ingredients: serves 4

4 slices of streaky bacon, chopped

4 eggs

Knob of butter for cooking

400g mixed salad leaves, washed and dried

4 spring onions, sliced lengthways

4 tablespoons olive oil

Juice of ½ lemon

Sea salt and freshly ground black pepper

Bacon and eggs is not just for breakfast. There is a growing trend towards intermittent fasting – extending the period each day when you don't eat anything. This can be helpful for weight and/or diabetes management and more people are adopting time restricted eating to avoid these conditions. We know a number of people who no longer have bacon and eggs for breakfast, but they have it for 'brunch' instead (a meal late morning/ early lunch time). If you have your first meal in the day even later, this is a wonderful lunch alternative to the classic breakfast).

Method

1 Fry the chopped bacon in a hot frying pan until nice and crispy. Then transfer to a warm plate.

2 Whisk the eggs. Add the butter to the frying pan and pour in the eggs. Cook for 4-5 minutes, as you would an omelette and then transfer to a warm plate.

3 Place the salad leaves in a bowl. Sprinkle the spring onions over the leaves. Slice the omelette into strips and place over the leaves. Sprinkle the bits of bacon on top.

4 For the dressing, pour the olive oil into the warm frying pan and add the lemon juice. Give it a good stir with a wooden spoon then season with salt and pepper. Pour the dressing over the salad. Toss together and serve immediately.

Warm chicken salad

Ingredients: serves 4 as a starter, 2 for a snack/lunch

4 tablespoons olive oil

2 breasts of chicken, cut into strips

Juice of ½ lemon

½ teaspoon mixed herbs

Sea salt and freshly ground black pepper

250g baby spinach, washed and roughly chopped

100g cherry tomatoes, quartered

4 spring onions, chopped

Method

1 Heat a small amount of olive oil in a frying pan and add the chicken strips. Cook for 5-6 minutes, turning occasionally, until they are cooked through and nicely browned. Remove from the heat and set aside.

2 Add the rest of the olive oil, lemon juice, herbs and seasoning to a mixing bowl and whisk.

3 Add the washed spinach, cherry tomatoes and spring onions to a salad bowl. Pour the dressing over the salad and toss.

4 Pour the chicken from the saucepan, including all the juices, over the salad. Toss lightly and serve immediately.

Egg Mayonnaise (v)

Ingredients: serves 4

4 tablespoons Natural Live Yoghurt (NLY)

1 teaspoon Dijon mustard

Salt and freshly ground pepper

4 eggs, hardboiled

This is another classic dish, made 'Harcombe friendly' by swapping out a few ingredients. We suggest you batch cook the eggs and then make the 'mayo' fresh as required.

Method

1 Mix the yoghurt, mustard, salt and pepper in a bowl.

2 Peel the eggs and roughly chop them into the bowl with the yoghurt mix.

3 Give the whole lot a good stir with a fork and then use as required.

TIP *For a quick Phase 2/3 lunch, fill an avocado with some egg mayonnaise (see photo – ours has some freshly ground pepper on top).*

Coronation chicken

Ingredients: serves 2

150g Natural Live Yoghurt (NLY)

1 teaspoon of Dijon mustard

4 dried apricots, chopped (optional)

200g pre-cooked chicken (you can use the scrapings off the carcase for this)

Sea salt and freshly ground pepper

4 iceberg lettuce leaves – 2 per serving

This is a great way to use up any bits of left-over chicken, as the appearance of the meat is disguised when it's mixed up with the other ingredients. It's also surprisingly rich and filling.

Method

1 In a mixing bowl, thoroughly mix the yoghurt, mustard, (optional) apricots and chicken and then season with salt and pepper.

2 Take 2 iceberg lettuce leaves and place one inside the other to create a small dish and spoon the mixture into the middle. Then, wrap the lettuce leaves around the chicken and yoghurt mixture and eat with your hands.

TIP *The apricots are not strictly Phase 1, so don't include them if you're doing a proper 5 day Phase 1. If you are doing an extended Phase 1, they won't hurt for one dish and they really do add to the flavour and texture. And/or if you are doing this dish for you and people not doing Phase 1 – include the apricots and make sure the other eaters get them!*

Curried chicken salad

Ingredients: serves 2

100ml Natural Live Yoghurt (NLY)

1 tablespoon curry powder

1 teaspoon chilli powder

Juice of ½ lemon

250g pre-cooked chicken

As with the Coronation chicken, this is a great way to use up any bits of left-over chicken, or you could cook some chicken just for the recipe.

Method

1 In a mixing bowl, thoroughly mix the NLY, curry powder, chilli powder and lemon juice. Leave to stand for 15 minutes and then add the pre-cooked chicken.

2 Leave the whole mixture to marinate for a minimum of 2 hours and then serve with a salad.

Butternut squash, carrot & ginger soup (v)

Ingredients: serves 4

Knob of butter for frying

1 medium onion, finely chopped

3 large carrots, approximately 250g, peeled and chopped

½ butternut squash, approximately 250g, peeled and chopped

Small piece of root ginger, peeled and grated

1 litre veggie stock

Sea salt and freshly ground black pepper

Zoë first tried this when we were in a London restaurant with friends. I can't vouch for the authenticity of the original recipe, but this version is 100% Phase 1, 'Harcombe friendly' and delicious as well!

Method

1 Melt the butter in a medium saucepan over a low heat. Add the chopped onion and sweat it over a low heat for about 5 minutes, until transparent.

2 Add the butternut squash and 2½ carrots to the saucepan. Pour in the stock and bring quickly to the boil. Reduce to simmer and pop on the lid. Simmer for about 20 minutes until the squash and carrots begin to soften.

3 Remove from the heat and allow to cool for a few minutes before blending with a hand blender to a smooth consistency.

4 Grate the remaining ½ carrot and stir into the soup, along with the grated ginger. Season to taste.

5 Bring the soup just back to the boil and serve hot.

TIP *This soup can also be chilled and kept in a fridge for 3-4 days, or frozen.*

Swede & turmeric soup (v)

Ingredients: serves 4

Knob of butter for frying

1 medium onion, finely chopped

1 swede, peeled and diced

3 small pieces fresh turmeric, peeled and chopped

1 litre vegetable stock

Sea salt and freshly ground black pepper

Turmeric is the new "best thing since sliced bread"! It can be bought and used as a root vegetable. It looks like a baby carrot with nobbly bits on and it is pretty pungent, so it is not to be eaten like carrots. It's used, as in this recipe, for flavour. Turmeric also comes as a spice – it's the one that makes curry yellow.

Turmeric has featured in Indian medicine for millennia. There is growing evidence of health benefit from the compounds in this plant. Curcumin is one such compound and this has anti-inflammatory and anti-oxidant effects. Curcumin is better absorbed when combined with black pepper, as we do here. Curcumin is also fat soluble and so is better absorbed when consumed with a fat meal. You may wish to follow this soup with a hearty meat or oily fish, therefore.

Method

1 Melt the butter in a medium saucepan over a low heat, add the chopped onion and sweat over a low heat for about 5 minutes, until transparent.

2 Add the diced swede and turmeric to the pan. Pour in the stock and bring quickly to the boil. Reduce to simmer and pop on the lid. Simmer for about 20 minutes until the swede just softens.

3 Remove from the heat and allow to cool for a few minutes before blending with a hand blender to a smooth consistency. Season to taste.

4 Bring the soup just back to the boil and serve hot.

Chef's salad

Ingredients: serves 4

4 eggs (optional)	4 sticks celery
Diced cubes of ham, chicken & other cold meat	4 spring onions
	Red & green pepper strips
1 iceberg lettuce	1 carrot, grated
14 cherry tomatoes	Olive oil or another dressing
1/2 cucumber	

This is a basic recipe – be your own chef and add in whatever you want – celeriac, beetroot, green beans – the more colour and vitamins the better.

Method:

1 Boil the eggs (place them in a saucepan of boiling water for 5-10 minutes, depending on how hard you like the yolks).

2 Dice the meat.

3 Chop the lettuce up quite finely and cover 4 plates with it. Slice the cherry tomatoes in half and place them around the edge of each plate.

4 Slice the cucumber, celery, spring onions and sprinkle these over the lettuce; add the pepper strips and grated carrot.

5 Quarter the hard-boiled eggs and arrange them on each plate. Add the meat cubes.

6 Add dressing to taste – olive oil is perfect, maybe with a squeeze of fresh lemon.

TIP *For Phase 2, add some diced hard cheese if you can tolerate dairy.*

TIP *Can be a vegetarian dish, if you leave out the meat.*

Chapter 6

Side dishes & sauces

Sauces and dips are great with crudités as an appetiser at dinner parties and they also give a fantastic boost to any packed lunch. We've taken some classic dips and made them 'Harcombe friendly' and have included a few others that we've created or come across on our travels. We usually make a few in advance, so that we have some variety throughout the week.

In this chapter:

- *Okra, tomato & coriander (v)*
- *Bubble & squeak (v)*
- *Roasted peppers (v)*
- *Mediterranean vegetables (v)*
- *Mediterranean style green beans (v)*
- *Broccoli, red onion & bacon*
- *Garlic roasted asparagus (v)*
- *Red mash (v)*
- *Green beans & tomatoes (v)*
- *Roast Brussel sprouts with bacon*
- *Butternut squash hash (v)*
- *Roast cauliflower with turmeric (v)*
- *Roast celeriac with curry butter (v)*
- *Cauliflower fried 'rice' (v)*
- *Chilli roast tomatoes (v)*
- *Stuffed marrow*
- *Cajun spice mix (can be v)*
- *Curried coleslaw (v)*

Okra, tomato & coriander (v)

Ingredients: 4 as a side dish

400g tin chopped tomatoes

Handful freshly chopped coriander (approximately 25g)

A big pinch of cumin

Sea salt and freshly ground pepper

500g okra, topped and tailed

Okra is also called "ladies fingers", as the shape of this vegetable is long and slender. Like all green vegetables, Okra is rich in vitamin C and naturally low in carbohydrate.

Method

1 Heat the tomatoes in a heavy pan and stir in half the chopped coriander, cumin, salt and pepper.

2 Bring to the boil and add the okra. Reduce the heat and simmer for 15 minutes, occasionally giving the mixture a stir.

3 Remove from the heat and stir in the remaining coriander. Transfer to a serving dish and serve warm, or chill and reheat as required.

Bubble & squeak (v)

Ingredients: 2-4 depending on your preferred vegetable portion size

Large knob of butter

1 onion, finely sliced

*500g, approximately, pre-cooked (leftover) vegetables –
broccoli, cauliflower, carrots, beans etc.*

Sea salt and freshly ground pepper

This is one of my (Andy's) favourite vegetable memories from my childhood. I don't know a vegetable that's not made better by re-cooking it with butter and a little salt and pepper.

Method

1 Melt the butter in a deep-frying pan and lightly fry the onion for about 5 minutes.

2 Add all the pre-cooked vegetable into the pan and give it a good stir. Cook for 15-20 minutes, stirring occasionally, until all the vegetables are reheated throughout and starting to brown in places

3 Season with generous helpings of sea salt and freshly ground pepper and serve immediately.

Roasted peppers (v)

Ingredients: serves 4

3 red peppers

2 green peppers

2 yellow peppers

50g sundried tomatoes

1 clove garlic, thinly sliced

50ml olive oil

2 tablespoons of lemon juice

Sea salt and freshly ground black pepper

Handful of freshly chopped basil

This is one of the most colourful dishes that you can make. We always provide it as one of the salad options with a Barbeque. When there is plenty of dark char-grilled meat, the colour of this dish brightens up the serving table.

Method

1 Pre-heat the oven to 200°C, 400°F, Gas 6.

2 Chop the peppers in half, deseed them and place the cleaned halves on a roasting tray. Pop in the oven and roast for about 45 minutes. Remove from the oven and allow to cool.

3 Thinly slice the sundried tomatoes and clove of garlic and set aside.

4 Once cooled, slice the roasted peppers and transfer to a serving dish. Add the sliced sundried tomatoes and garlic.

5 Whisk the olive oil and lemon juice in a mixing bowl and season well. Pour the dressing over the sliced peppers, tomatoes and garlic and stir well. Cover and set aside to marinate for a few hours.

6 Just before serving, give the mixture a final stir and sprinkle with chopped basil.

Mediterranean vegetables (v)

Ingredients: serves many

Olive oil for cooking

1 red onion, roughly chopped

2 cloves garlic, roughly bashed

½ fresh fennel, coarsely chopped

1 green pepper, deseeded and chopped

1 yellow pepper, deseeded and chopped

2 courgettes, sliced lengthways in quarter, then chopped

2 carrots, chopped into 1cm lengths

2 x 400g tins tomatoes, chopped

Sea salt and freshly ground pepper

Healthy dash of Tabasco (optional)

This is a delicious vegetable dish, a bit like a ratatouille, that you can make in bulk and use as you go. It's also a quick and simple dish to make in advance, which saves a lot of messing around on a party day, as it's one fewer dish to worry about.

Method

1 In a heavy based casserole dish, lightly fry the onion, garlic and fennel in some olive oil for 2-3 minutes. Add all the other chopped vegetables and give them a good stir.

2 Pour over the chopped tomatoes, season well, including the optional Tabasco, and give the whole stew a good stir. Bring to the boil then reduce the heat to simmer. Pop on the casserole dish lid and cook on a low heat for about 20 minutes.

3 If you are going to serve immediately, cook for an additional 10 minutes, until the carrots are tender. If you're cooking in advance, allow to cool, and keep in a cool place until required. Then reheat quickly and simmer for 10 minutes until warmed through.

Mediterranean style green beans (v)

Ingredients: serves 4

2 tablespoons olive oil

1 large onion, finely sliced

2 garlic cloves, finely sliced

6 large ripe plum tomatoes, coarsely chopped

450g green beans, sliced lengthways

Handful of black olives, stoned

150ml vegetable stock

2 teaspoons lemon juice

Sea salt and freshly ground pepper

You'll often see this served as a side dish in the Mediterranean. It's a great way to jazz up the plain old green bean.

Method

1 In a deep frying pan, lightly fry the onion and garlic in the olive oil for 2-3 minutes. Add the tomatoes, beans and olives and pour in the stock and lemon juice. Bring to a simmer and cook on a low heat for 20 minutes.

2 Transfer to a warmed serving dish, season to taste and serve immediately. This dish can also be served cold as a delicious accompaniment to cold meats.

Broccoli, red onion & bacon

Ingredients: serves 4

3 slices of streaky bacon, sliced

Large knob of butter

1 red onion, finely sliced

300g broccoli, part-cooked

Sea salt and freshly ground pepper

This recipe uses part-cooked broccoli. This makes it perfect for using up leftovers or part-cook from fresh by covering with some wet kitchen roll and cooking in a microwave on high for 2 minutes.

Method

1 In a deep frying pan, fry the bacon in its own fat until it starts to crisp.

2 Add the butter and red onion, give it all a good stir and cook for a further 3 minutes.

3 Add the part-cooked broccoli and give another stir. Cook for a further 10 minutes, stirring occasionally so that the broccoli gets nicely coated with butter and bacon fat and cooked evenly.

4 Transfer to a warm serving dish and serve immediately.

Garlic roasted asparagus (v)

Ingredients: serves 4

400g asparagus

1 tablespoon olive oil

1 clove garlic, finely sliced

Sea salt and freshly ground pepper

Asparagus is a uniquely tasty vegetable made even more special by quickly roasting it with garlic. This is ideal as an accompanying vegetable when you have the oven on anyway for your main meal.

Method

1 Pre-heat the oven to 200°C, 400°F, Gas 6.

2 Prepare the asparagus by breaking off the woody ends.

3 Spread the asparagus on a large roasting tray. Dribble the olive oil over the asparagus and sprinkle over the sliced garlic. Toss all together so that the asparagus is well coated with the oil. Season with salt and pepper.

4 Pop in the oven and roast for about 20 minutes until lightly brown. Remove from the oven and allow to cool for a few minutes. Serve warm or at room temperature.

Red mash (v)

Ingredients: serves many

300g swede

300g celeriac

300g carrots

300g parsnips

300g beetroot

½ litre vegetable stock

Sea salt and freshly ground pepper

(Vary the quantities to suit your taste, or whatever root vegetables you have)

Did you ever have mashed parsnips as a child? If you did, this is one step better and it provides a vivid red colour to accompany roast meat. The colour is so striking, it never fails to get a comment and then a query: "how did you make that?"

Method

1 Peel and dice all the vegetables and place them in a large saucepan, with approximately 2 litre capacity.

2 Pour about ½ litre of stock over the vegetables, so that they are barely covered and bring them quickly to the boil. Reduce the heat and simmer for about 25 minutes, until the vegetables are just turning soft.

3 Remove from the heat and allow to cool for 10 minutes. Then blitz with a hand blender to get a nice smooth mash.

4 Season liberally, give a quick stir and serve immediately.

TIP *If you leave the beetroot out, you have orange mash!*

Green beans & tomatoes (v)

Ingredients: serves 4

1 tablespoon olive oil

1 clove garlic, finely sliced

450g green beans, topped and tailed

400g tin tomatoes, chopped

½ teaspoon mixed herbs

Sea salt and freshly ground pepper

Method

1 Lightly fry the garlic in the olive oil for 2 minutes until it just softens. Stir in the beans and cook for a further 2 minutes.

2 Pour the chopped tomatoes over the beans and sprinkle the mixed herbs over the tomatoes. Give the mixture a good stir and bring to the boil. Reduce the heat so that the mixture is simmering and cook for 10 minutes, stirring occasionally until the beans just begin to soften.

3 Season with salt and pepper, give the mix a final stir and transfer to a warmed serving dish.

Roast brussels sprouts with bacon

Ingredients: serves 4

300g Brussels sprouts

1 tablespoon olive oil

3 slices streaky bacon, sliced

1 clove garlic, thinly sliced

Knob of butter

Sea salt and freshly ground pepper

With memories of over-cooked, mushy and tasteless sprouts for school dinners, I (Andy) was a take-it-or-leave-it person when it came to this classic vegetable. Then I discovered roasting them, and my life has not been the same since.

Method

1 Pre-heat the oven to 200°C, 400°F, Gas 6.

2 Chop off the hard stalk from the sprouts and slice each one in half. Spread them out on a roasting tray and sprinkle them with olive oil. Toss the sprouts to make sure that they are all covered with oil. Pop the tray in the top of the oven for 30-40 minutes, until they begin to brown.

3 Remove from the oven and allow to steam-off for a few minutes.

4 Meanwhile, fry the bacon in its own fat in a hot frying pan, stirring occasionally, until the bacon is crispy.

5 Add the butter to the bacon and stir well. Then add the roasted sprouts and stir well. Cook for a further 2-3 minutes, stirring frequently, until all the ingredients are well mixed together and warmed through.

6 Season well, give a final stir and transfer to a warmed serving dish. Serve hot.

Butternut squash hash (v)

Ingredients: serves 4

3 tablespoons olive oil

1 clove garlic, thinly sliced

1 onion, quartered

1 butternut squash, approximately 1kg, peeled and diced

Sea salt for seasoning

This dish may be a little too 'carby' for some, but it's a delicious homely addition to any roast dinner for those who are OK with starchy vegetables. You can also chill and reheat another day (like 'bubble-and-squeak').

Method

1 Pre-heat the oven to 200°C, 400°F, Gas 6.

2 Heat the olive oil in a large frying pan and lightly fry the garlic and onion until they become transparent.

3 Add the butternut squash cubes to the pan and fry for a further 5 minutes, stirring occasionally.

4 Transfer to a roasting dish and pop in the oven for 30 minutes. Remove from the oven to give everything a good stir and then return to the oven for a further 30 minutes.

5 Just before serving, sprinkle generously with sea salt, give the ingredients a final stir and transfer to a warmed serving dish.

Roast cauliflower with turmeric (v)

Ingredients: serves 4

1 cauliflower, chopped into florets

2 tablespoons of coconut oil

1 tablespoon dried turmeric

Generous pinch of sea salt

Some sprigs of fresh coriander to garnish

Method

1 Pre-heat the oven to 200°C, 400°F, Gas 6.

2 Mix the coconut oil, turmeric and sea salt in a small mixing bowl.

3 Spread the cauliflower florets on a roasting tray and spoon the olive oil mix over the florets. Toss the florets to make sure that they are well covered with the oil.

4 Pop in the oven and roast for 30 minutes. Remove to turn the florets and then return to the oven for a further 20 minutes, until the florets have turned a nice brown.

5 Transfer to a warmed serving dish and garnish with some fresh coriander sprigs.

Roast celeriac with curry butter (v)

Ingredients: serves 4

1 celeriac, approximately 750g

75g butter

1 tablespoon curry powder

½ teaspoon fenugreek seeds

½ teaspoon black mustard seeds

Generous pinch of sea salt

Method

1 Pre-heat the oven to 175°C, 350°F, Gas 4.

2 Peel, or cut away, the outer skin of the celeriac and cut into "chips". Place them on a baking tray.

3 Melt the butter in a saucepan. Add the curry powder and seeds and heat to release the flavour for approximately 30 seconds. DO NOT allow the butter mixture to burn.

4 Pour the butter over the celeriac and mix the chips in the butter until they are fully coated.

5 Pop the chips in the oven and roast for 50-60 minutes, turning occasionally. The chips will not be crisp; they will remain deliciously chewy.

TIP *A simple alternative to celeriac is to slice a cauliflower into 'steaks', pour over the butter and roast for 40 minutes, turning at half-way.*

Cauliflower fried 'rice' (v)

Ingredients: serves 2

1 large cauliflower

Cauliflower rice has become a trendy side dish in the low carb world. It's easy to make and is a tasty and healthy alternative to the more starchy rice. Caution – cauliflower rice can smell a bit 'weird' as it's cooking, but it doesn't taste like it smells as soon as it is served. Cauliflower rice has become so mainstream; you can even buy pre-prepared options in most supermarkets. Why pay the premium when making it is so easy?

Method

To prepare: remove all the green leaves from the cauliflower and cut it into quarters. Take a grater and simply grate the cauliflower to make 'rice'.

Here are two simple ways to cook:

One option is to lightly fry in a small amount of olive or coconut oil for about 5 minutes, stirring frequently.

Another option is to place the 'rice' in a mixing bowl, cover tightly with cling film and microwave on high for 2 minutes.

The first option will produce a drier rice and the second a more traditional moist rice. Both are delicious for mopping up the gravy in stews and casseroles.

Chilli roast tomatoes (v)

Ingredients: serves 4

400g cherry tomatoes

4 tablespoons olive oil

1-2 teaspoons chilli flakes

Method

1 Pre-heat the oven to 175°C, 350°F, Gas 4.

2 Put the tomatoes on a roasting dish and drizzle the olive oil over them.

3 Sprinkle the chilli flakes over the tomatoes and pop the dish in the pre-heated oven and roast for 30 minutes, until the tomatoes start to brown.

4 Chill and serve as required.

TIP *The oil mixed with the tomato juices is sweet and hot and is a deliciously simple dressing for a green salad.*

Stuffed marrow

Ingredients: serves 4

1 marrow, cut into 6cm thick slices

2 tablespoons olive oil

4 slices streaky bacon, chopped

1 medium onion, finely chopped

2 cloves garlic, crushed

2 sprigs fresh thyme

Marrow is a bland vegetable when just boiled in water, but when it's stuffed and roasted like in this recipe, it's a delicious addition to any simply roast meat or fish. It's also great value, as not many people know what to do with it. Give it a go!

Method

1 Preheat an oven to 200°C, 400°F, Gas 6

2 Scoop out the flesh from the middle of the 6cm slices and coarsely chop the flesh. place the marrow slices on a baking tray that's lightly greased with olive oil.

3 Fry the bacon in a frying pan for about 5 minutes until the fat starts to brown. Add the onion and garlic and fry in the bacon fat for a further 2 minutes. Add the flesh from the marrow and cook for a further 5 minutes, stirring frequently.

4 Scoop the mixture from the frying pan into the marrow slices, pressing the mixture down firmly into the marrow. Please the stuffed marrows into the oven and roast for 30 minutes.

5 Serve hot.

TIP *For Phase 2, sprinkle some grated cheese on the marrow slices before roasting to add some additional flavour and texture.*

Cajun spice mix (can be v)

Ingredients

1 teaspoon coriander seeds

1 teaspoon cumin seeds

1 teaspoon fennel seeds

½ teaspoon cardamom seeds

1 teaspoon black peppercorns

2 teaspoons dried oregano

1 teaspoon dried basil

1 teaspoon paprika

½ teaspoon chilli powder

½ teaspoon garlic salt

We've included this recipe, as it is one of the all-time favourites from our main recipe book and because it is so flexible. Rub it onto vegetables, fish or meat before grilling, roasting or barbecuing to add the most delicious flavours. No 'Harcombe Friendly' recipe book would be complete without it.

Method

1 Put the coriander, cumin, fennel and cardamom seeds together with the black peppercorns in a pestle and mortar and crush them well.

2 Transfer the crushed seeds to a mixing bowl and add the remaining ingredients. Mix everything together thoroughly.

3 Rub the mixture into steak, lamb, pork, chicken, fish, aubergine, onions and anything else that you would grill, roast or barbecue and cook as you would normally.

TIP *Make in a larger batch and keep in an airtight container to have a quick fix spice mix handy at all times.*

Curried coleslaw (v)

Ingredients: serves 4

250g Natural Live Yoghurt (NLY)

Big pinch sea salt

1-2 teaspoons curry powder

1 teaspoon chilli powder

1 large carrot, grated

1/4 celeriac, grated

Our yoghurt based coleslaw is always a hit at our house and this version has an extra little twist, and bite.

Method

1 Put the NLY, salt, curry powder and clilli powder in a large mixing bowl and stir to a smooth consistency.

2 Stir in the grated carrot and celeriac and give a good stir until they are well covered by the yoghurt mix.

3 Serve as desired.

Chapter 7

Phase 1 summary

What you can eat and drink in Phase 1

Meats:

As much fresh, unprocessed, meat, as you need. This can be white meat and birds (chicken, duck, goose, guinea fowl, pheasant, quail, rabbit and turkey), or, red meat (bacon, beef, fresh ham, lamb, pork, veal and venison). Buying from the (local) butcher will be best for food quality, food miles and cooking tips.

Fish:

As much fresh or tinned fish as you need - no smoked fish. This can include white fish like cod, haddock, halibut, plaice, turbot and whiting. It can include oily fish like anchovies, mackerel, pilchards, salmon, tuna and trout. It can also include shellfish and seafood like clams, crab, lobster, mussels, oysters and prawns.

Eggs:

As many eggs as you need (chicken, duck or any others you like).

Brown rice, quinoa or oats:

You can have up to 50 grams (dry weight - before cooking) of brown rice per day, or brown rice cereal, or brown rice pasta, or quinoa or porridge oats. If you are vegetarian, you can have up to 150 grams.

Salads and vegetables:

You can have as many salads and vegetables as you need, except mushrooms and potatoes.

Natural Live (bio) Yoghurt (NLY):

We think of Phase 1 as dairy-free, as milk, cream and cheese are all excluded. Natural Live Yoghurt is allowed and The Harcombe Diet books explain why. Phase 1 was designed as the optimal diet to overcome three conditions that drive food cravings. Many people with lactose intolerance are fine with NLY and NLY is helpful to overcome one of the conditions. NLY is also great for variety and enjoyment during Phase 1. On balance, therefore, this was included.

Tofu:

This is a vegetarian protein alternative, which is fine in Phase 1, provided that it doesn't contain added ingredients.

Drinks:

You can drink as much bottled water (still or sparkling) or tap water as you like during Phase 1. You can drink herbal teas, decaffeinated tea and decaffeinated coffee.

No alcohol, fruit juices, soft drinks, canned drinks, caffeinated products or milk. Just to be clear, you can't have milk or cream in tea or coffee on Phase 1.

Note:

Don't eat anything that is not on the list above on Phase 1. No fruit, no wheat or grains (other than the brown rice/oat options listed), no white rice, no sugar, no cakes, no biscuits, no confectionery, no cheese, no pickled or processed foods. Don't eat anything to which you are allergic - obviously.

We've included a handy summary of Phase on the opposite page.

The Harcombe Diet®

www.theharcombedietclub.com

Phase 1 Summary.

1) Eat real food. We have included many examples on the 'allowed' list below. Fish swim in the sea; fish fingers don't – you'll get the idea.

2) Eat three times a day. *Ideally* get into the habit of eating three (or two) main meals a day, with snacks only if you are genuinely hungry.

3) Eat as much as you need from the allowed list. Don't eat anything that is not on this list – no fruit, no other grains, no milk, no cheese etc.

Phase 1 Allowed List.

Vegetables & Salads. Alfalfa, Artichoke, Asparagus, Aubergine, Bamboo shoots, Bean sprouts, Beetroot, Broccoli, Brussels sprouts, Bok choy, Cabbage (any), Carrots, Cauliflower, Celeriac, Celery, Chicory, Chillies (any), Courgettes, Cucumber, Dandelion, Endive, Fennel , Garlic, Green beans, Kale, Leeks, Lettuce (any), Mange tout, Marrow, Mustard greens, Okra, Onions, Parsnip, Peas, Peppers (any), Pumpkin, Radish, Rocket, Salsify, Shallots, Sorrel, Spinach, Spring onions, Squashes, Swiss chard, Swede, Turnip, Watercress, Water chestnuts.

Herbs & Spices. Basil, Bay leaves, Caraway, Cardamom, Chervil, Chives, Cinnamon, Cloves, Coriander, Cumin, Dill, Ginger, Marjoram, Mint, Nutmeg, Oregano, Paprika, Parsley, Pepper, Rosemary, Saffron, Sage, Salt, Tarragon, Thyme, Turmeric.

White Fish. Cod, Haddock, Halibut, Plaice, Turbot, Whiting.

Seafood. Clams, Crab, Lobster, Mussels, Oysters, Prawns, Winkles.

Oily Fish. Anchovies, Mackerel, Pilchards, Salmon, Tuna, Trout.

White Meat & Birds. Chicken, Duck, Goose, Guinea Fowl, Pheasant, Quail, Rabbit, Turkey.

Red Meat. Bacon, Beef, Gammon, Ham, Lamb, Pork, Veal, Venison.

Other. Eggs, Natural Live (Bio) Yoghurt, Tofu.

Misc. Butter, Olives, Olive oil, Tomatoes.

Drinks. Water, Herbal teas, Decaf tea & coffee.

The only food limited in quantity is brown rice/quinoa/plain oats of which you can have 50g dry weight or 150g if you are vegetarian, per day.
If you are allergic or intolerant to any 'allowed' foods, clearly avoid these.

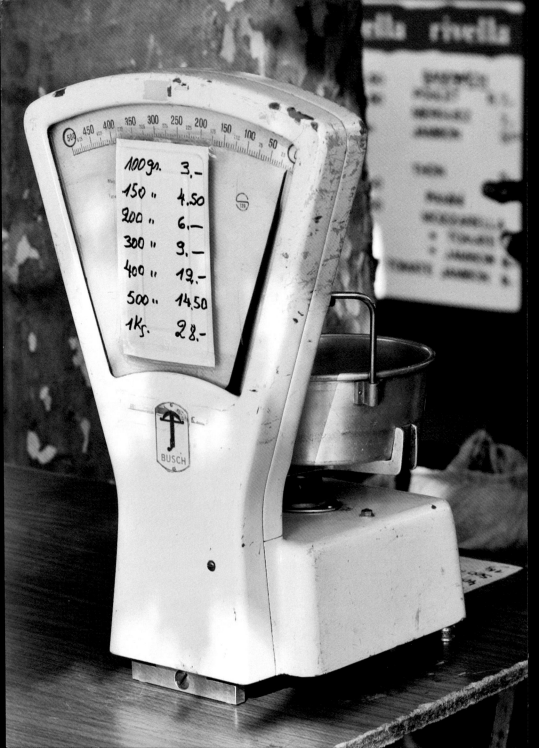

100 gr.	3.—
150 "	4.50
200 "	6.—
300 "	9.—
400 "	12.—
500 "	14.50
1 kg.	28.—

Useful tables and measures

When we list weights or volumes for ingredients, these are always pre-cooked weights and volumes. Hence "100g brown rice" on the ingredients list will be 100g of brown rice grains straight from the packet – the weight will approximately double when cooked for this particular ingredient. 200g of spinach, on the contrary, will reduce in weight a little, and substantially in volume, when it is cooked.

Most recipes are designed to serve 1, 2 or 4 people. Please adjust the quantities to suit your family size and/or to make some leftovers for another meal.

To make the recipes easy to follow, we have listed all the ingredients in the order that you will use them.

Many of our recipes refer to a large frying pan. This can be a wok – whatever you normally use to fry things with minimal olive oil.

If there is anything you don't like in a recipe, leave it out or swap it for something similar (one spice for another, one vegetable for another etc). Recipes are meant to be adapted to suit your tastes.

Please check any tins or packets for unnecessary ingredients. You'll find sugar in tins of vegetables and pulses unless you're careful. Tins of tomatoes usually have citric acid as an added ingredient – this is fine as a preservative. Stock cubes are virtually impossible to get without sugar (an 'ose') somewhere on the list. Get one with any nasties as far down the list as possible and then don't worry. The cube is usually about a centimetre squared and it ends up being added to a lot of liquid in a dish serving four people, so the amount you end up with is absolutely tiny.

Tinned vegetables are fine. Tinned fish is especially healthy, if you choose the options with bones and skin left in – that's where the vitamin D is most concentrated. Frozen vegetables are also fine as an alternative to fresh vegetables and useful to keep in stock.

We always recommend Natural Live Yoghurt (also called bio on some labels) and this is important for gut health.

We've used the metric system for weights and temperatures and have also included an imperial conversion where appropriate.

We list Fahrenheit, Celsius and gas marks on every recipe to make sure that the setting for your own oven is always to hand, without the need to convert.

For completeness, here is a useful reminder of the various conversions that you may need while using this book.

Oven temperature conversions:

Fahrenheit	Centigrade	Gas mark	Description
225 – 275 f	110 – 135 c	0 – 1	Very Cool
300 – 325 f	150 – 165 c	2 – 3	Cool
350 – 375 f	175 – 190 c	4 – 5	Moderate
400 – 425 f	200 – 220 c	6 – 7	Hot
450 – 475 f	230 – 245 c	8 – 9	Very Hot

Conversion table for weight: Metric to imperial

Metric	Metric	Imperial	Imperial
g	kg	oz	lbs
100	0.1	3.5	0.22
250	0.25	8.75	0.55
500	0.5	17.5	1.1
1000	1	35	2.2

Conversion table for volumes and liquids:

USA Cups	Universal Tablespoons	Imperial Fluid oz	Imperial Pints	Metric ml	Other
1/16	1			15	= 3 teasp
1/8	2	1		30	
1/4	4	2	1/8	60	
1/2	8	4	1/4	120	
3/4	12	6	1/6	180	
1	16	8	1/2	240	
2	32	16	1	480	
4.2	68	34	2.1	1000	= 1 litre

Index

Other books by Zoë Harcombe:

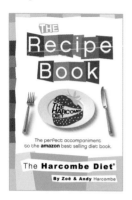

The Harcombe Diet:
The Recipe Book

Real food; great taste; optimal health – that's what The Harcombe Diet® is all about and here's how to do it. With over 100 recipes for Phase 1, another 100 for Phase 2 and some seriously special Phase 3 cheats, this is the ultimate diet-recipe book. If you want to eat well, lose weight and gain health – this is a must for your kitchen shelf.

ISBN 978-1-907797-07-1

The Harcombe Diet:
Stop Counting Calories
& Start Losing Weight

You've tried every diet under the sun. You've lost weight and put it back on. The more you diet, the more you crave food. You've given up hope of being slim. This book explains why. Count calories & end up a food addict. Stop Counting Calories& Start Losing Weight!

ISBN 978-1-907797-11-8

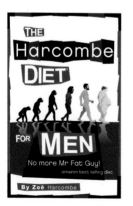

The Harcombe Diet for Men:
No More Mr Fat Guy

Men want to lose weight too - fast - and they won't go hungry. They want steak, pasta, cheese and the good things in life, including wine. They'll exercise if they want to; they won't count calories and they want all the answers in just a few pages...
So here it is - The Harcombe Diet® for men!

ISBN 978-1-907797-12-5

The Harcombe Diet Lunchbox Recipes

This book will show you how to knock up quick & healthy lunches, for anywhere, anytime. With our mix & make formula, you could create 8,000 different lunch box variations. Enough to keep even the most demanding palettes satisfied. If you want to eat real, healthy food while out and about, this is a great addition to your bookshelf, whether you're on a diet or not.

ISBN 978-1-907797-45-3

The Obesity Epidemic
What caused it? How can we stop it?

"The Obesity Epidemic is the most comprehensive demolition job on the arrogance and ignorance of the health profession I have ever read". Barry Groves. Author *Trick and Treat: How 'healthy eating' is making us ill*.

ISBN 978-1-907797-00-2

Looking for diet and health support?
Find out more about The Harcombe Diet® at:

www.theharcombedietclub.com

www.theharcombedietclub.com

Eat naturally, Move naturally
Lose weight, Gain health